PICTURESQUE
INDIA

PICTURESQUE INDIA

A JOURNEY IN EARLY PICTURE POSTCARDS (1896–1947)

Sangeeta and Ratnesh Mathur

NIYOGI
BOOKS

Published by

NIYOGI BOOKS

Block D, Building No. 77,
Okhla Industrial Area, Phase-I,
New Delhi-110 020, INDIA
Tel: 91-11-26816301, 26818960
Email: niyogibooks@gmail.com
Website: www.niyogibooksindia.com

Text and images © Sangeeta and Ratnesh Mathur

Editor: Upama Biswas
Design: Shashi Bhushan Prasad

ISBN: 978-93-85285-91-2
Publication: 2018

Printed at: Niyogi Offset Pvt. Ltd., New Delhi, India

To

God Chitragupta

Who so benevolently revealed many a *gupt* (hidden) *chitras*

(pictures) to us duing the course of our journey

CONTENTS

PREFACE

For centuries, India, the land of fables, has been imagined by people from far-off lands. Greek geographers and explorers had begun writing about India around 500 BCE. From the Hellenic Greek period, references to India are to be found in at least seven books, such as Megasthenes's *Indica* written around 320 BCE and Strabo's *Geographica* compiled over many years beginning 65 BCE. Later, Ptolemy, in his 2nd CE work *Geographia*, describes India as the fabled land, farthest away from Europe. The entire geography beyond Pars (Persia) and below Tartaria and Chin (China) was labeled "India". In all likelihood, the name India itself emerges from these descriptions of Greek and Persian travellers, explorers and traders who had experienced the land beyond the Indus, known as Sindhu in ancient Indian lore.

By the 15th century, as the European race for the sea route to India began, the European imagination of India turned into an obsession. India, or its variants in different European tongues—*Inde/Indies/Indika*, was best captured in the shapes and boundaries of the earliest maps made by their cartographers. With the European discovery of the Americas in 1492, two Indias emerged—"West Indies" and "East Indies". West Indies was renamed "America" in April 1507 by the cartographer Martin Waldseemuller, on the basis of the writings and letters that he had received from the early explorer of the West Indies, Amerigo Vespucci, describing the new-found land in much detail. This term has not, in fact, disappeared entirely as it continues to describe a bunch of Caribbean islands even today.

On the other hand, East Indies continued to describe today's South-East Asia, well into the era of European scientific cartography, or upto the beginning of the 19th century. Australia was discovered and named in 1770, and in the postcolonial nations of today, we do not just have the modern India of 1947, but also the large archipelago of 13,000 islands, which named itself Indonesia, a combination of *India* and *Nesia*, meaning islands in Greek. Also, in 16th- to 18th-century European cartography today's India and the entire South-East Asia region was divided into two parts: "India intra Gangem" or India within the Ganges and "India extra Gangem" or India outside the Ganges. The extra Gangem land stretched all the way to modern Vietnam, which had been titled "Indo-China" by Europeans earlier.

Further, by the 15th and 16th centuries, with Germany able to mass produce paper prints, the "Route to India" maps and the picture of an Indian elephant and a one-horned rhinoceros emerged as some of the most popular early visual prints in Europe.

World Philately Fair, 2008, Prague

Meanwhile, as the book and print making ownership in Europe moved from an elite few to the masses, the focus of the written word stayed, of course, on the Bible.

The printing and even the papermaking technology had entered Europe from China, where printing of pictures had begun as early as the 9th century. Initially, they used woodblock printing for pictures, but by the 11th century, China had invented the "movable type" printing mechanism for printing texts. The subject of China's earliest printing on paper, in both text and woodblock pictures, was mainly Buddhist teachings from India, printed in the world's oldest surviving book, *The Diamond Sutra*, printed in the year 868 CE, nearly 600 years before the Gutenberg Bible was printed in Germany. The Sanskrit title of this oldest book, *Vajracchedikā Prajñāpāramitā Sūtra*, translates to "Diamond cutting perfection of Wisdom". This prized first edition contained woodcut pictures of the Buddha teaching his disciples at different locations in India.

We started collecting antiquarian maps and prints of India in the mid-1990s from shops and auction houses in India and on our travels abroad. We were well aware of the European fascination of the sea route to India during the "age of exploration", since this had been well documented in cartography. In 2003, we relocated to Central Europe for a few years on a work assignment. This opened new windows for us in our print collecting hobbies. We, of course, started seeing India in a different light—as non-residents—and as we searched for old Indian prints in Central Europe's antiquarian bookshops and weekend hobby club gatherings, we came across a treasure trove of early photographs of India, printed as "Picture Postcards" and posted by Europeans back home from their travels to India.

Austria, The Czech and Slovak Republics, Hungary and Germany were all part of the Austro-Hungarian Empire, when in 1869, in the Empire's capital, Vienna, Dr Emanuel Hermann conceptualised the "postcard". The "Golden Era" of the picture postcard (1890–1918) marks the beginning of their usage, leading upto to an explosion in the usage of the medium lasting until the end of World War I in 1918. During this phase, a cheaper form without pictures, known as the

"Correspondence Card" or just "Postcard", had been introduced in British India and in many Indian princely states. While this became the popular product within India, Europeans themselves largely switched to the more expensive "Picture Postcard", sending these pictures in large numbers to family and friends, sharing the visuals captured by the early photographers in India. Within Europe, the hobby of collecting postcards, which began in the Golden Era, came to be known as *Deltiology*. The practice has somehow continued into these internet boom years. Monthly weekend collectors' club meetings for stamp and postcard collectors still take place in most central European towns. We joined these clubs in 2003 and thus began a "journey of collecting and comprehending" which hasn't yet ended. By 2007, we had graduated to attending global meets of philatelists and deltiologists.

Over the past 15 years, it has been an enriching experience to build our own collection of over 4,500 rare picture postcards of India. Many postcard enthusiasts around the globe have contributed to this collection—Mr Deepak Jain of All Arts, New Delhi, and Mr Baru, at Dominikanska Street, Brno, Czech Republic, have helped immensely with their contributions. Published between 1896 and 1947, these postcards feature early pictures of more than 350 towns of India and Pakistan. Travelling through India with these pictures and related travel books of the same period, namely guidebooks by John Murray & Co. and Thomas Cook & Co., British India tourism and railway brochures and travelogues by various other writers, has opened doors to an alternative history of India—a visual one.

It is quite obvious to us now that the European fascination for the "Picture of India" didn't just end with the 15th- and 16th-century prints of the elephant but continued all the way, well into the years of the television. Now, deep into the internet years as mobile-phone photography and instant sharing of selfies on social media explodes, the picture postcard is clearly in its final years. But while town after town in Europe has recorded its visual history in books with the help of picture postcard reprints, no book has yet been published on the picture postcards of India. While a few books on early photography and on the colonial history of Indian towns such as Bombay (Mumbai), Calcutta (Kolkata)

and Dehradun have occasionally reprinted some postcard images, the story of the Indian picture postcard largely remains untold.

With this book, we hope to make a beginning. We have selected some 550 postcards from our collection to answer the question: What would it be like to travel across India a hundred years back? Pictures have been selected and arranged on the basis of travel routes of that time. This is a pictorial journey and not a before and after comparison. To those who know the land routes and follow the trail, the pictures should provide the answers. Our focus in the book is mainly topographical. Therein lies the challenge. Even without Pakistan and Bangladesh today, the subcontinent of India with its 29 states, 8,000 towns and 6,00,000 villages has a diversity and size too large for one person in one lifetime to know or to photograph or to paint or travel to. Even the 90-odd postcard photography and publishing studios catalogued in this book and the selection of 550 pictures of 130 locations is inadequate. Eventually, like the European and American historians and urban planners have already done, and many towns in South-East Asia have begun to do, we hope that picture postcard reprint books on each of India's large towns, too, will soon get published. Most of the picture postcard printers and publishers of India specialised in publishing pictures of the parts of India around them. Much research has gone into summarising the history of these early printers and publishers. This book is not definitive, but just a beginning, which should provide the readers the necessary impetus to dig deeper and search for more treasures of the country's visual history. After all, every picture does, indeed, tell a story.

Sangeeta and Ratnesh Mathur

INTRODUCTION

India: The Picturesque and the Colonial

> *Seeing comes before words. The child looks and recognizes before it can speak.*
> *But, there is also another sense in which seeing comes before words. It is seeing*
> *which establishes our place in the surrounding world; we explain that world with*
> *words, but words can never undo the fact that we are surrounded by it. The relation*
> *between what we see and what we know is never settled.*

> —John Berger, *Ways of Seeing*

During the 18th and 19th centuries, many British landscape artists arrived in India to sketch and paint its imposing forts and richly decorated palaces, temples, pagodas and mosques. They captured the grandeur of the Mughal cities in decline, the new colonial settlements in growth and, of course, the Himalayas with the flow of the Ganga and other rivers from the hills to the oceans and bays. Besides these topographical views, the appearance, attires, culture and customs of the diverse people of India were fascinating subjects to paint and share with Europeans back home, filling in their curiosity of this far-off land. The fabled flora and fauna continued to be painted till much later, taken up as a popular subject by the Englishwomen arriving in India by the late 19th century. Pioneer landscape artists like William Hodges, Thomas and William Daniell, Charles D'Oyly, William Simpson and James Baillie Fraser travelled across India exploring and sketching remote regions. Their work created a sensation in Europe, being much in demand between the years 1770–1880. This pushed the emergence of new picture printing techniques towards mass production, beginning with Prague-based Alois Senefelder's innovation in lithography in 1796. The original paintings were multiplied as engravings and lithography prints for sale in the European markets and, over the years, numerous "illustrated travelogues of India", which included these engravings and lithographic pictures, were published, becoming extremely popular. The following image titled "Shooting tiger from platform" is from the 1832 book titled *Pen and Pencil Sketches: Being the Journal of a Tour in India* by Captain Mundy, published by John Murray. Nearly a hundred years later, a coloured lithographic postcard printed in England titled "Tiger Shooting" features an identical image to the one that had been sketched for the travelogue.

Sketch titled "Shooting tiger from platform" from Captain Mundy's book

Shooting Tiger from platform.   London. Pub.d by John Murray. April 1832.

Tiger Shooting

In 1768, the English artist and writer William Gilpin in his book *Three Essays: on Picturesque Beauty; on Picturesque Travel; and on Sketching Landscapes* defined the term "picturesque" in so many words:

> Disputes about beauty might perhaps be involved in less confusion, if a distinction were established, which certainly exists, between such objects as are *beautiful*, and such as are *picturesque*, between those which please the eye in their *natural state*; and those which please from some quality, capable of being *illustrated in painting*.

The landscape artists who travelled across India focused exclusively on the picturesque. They even used a pre-photography gadget, the camera obscura, as a tool to edit, alter proportions and facilitate capturing the picturesque. The accompanying text and travel narratives to these picturesque paintings, published as books, further created an enigma of an Oriental wonderland. In 1850, a spirited Welsh travel writer, Lady Fanny Parkes, published a book titled *Wanderings of a Pilgrim in Search of the Picturesque: During Four and Twenty years in the East with Revelations of Life in the Zenana.* In 1890, W.S. Caine came out with a beautiful book titled *Picturesque India: A Handbook for European Travellers.* For the pictures, he had hired 3 illustrators in London—John Pedder, H. Sheppard Dale and H.H. Stanton—to draw over 250 picturesque sketches, using the photographs of Bourne & Shepherd, Calcutta; Frith & Co., Reigate; Lala Deen Dayal of Indore and Nicholas & Co., Madras (Chennai).

With the invention of the camera, early photographers of India from the 1850s, such as Robert Gill, Felice Beato, R.B. Oakley, Linnaeus Tripe, Captains T. Biggs and E.D. Lyon, to the prominent photographers of the 1890s, such as John Burke, Lala Deen Dayal, Samuel Bourne, Charles Shepherd, Johnston and Hoffmann and T.A. Rust, began replacing the landscape artists, but their emphasis continued to be on the picturesque. Felice Beato, who had reached Lucknow and Kanpur just after the 1857 War of Independence, even stage-managed his war photographs using actors to create photos with the right aesthetics, not too different from the way many photographers use the Photoshop software today.

LEFT:
A 1902 postcard, sent from Bombay to Constantinople, titled "A Fair Exchange", lithographed by W. Cooper at Bombay.

Asking for Alms

A later-day, evidently stage-managed photographic postcard titled "Asking for Alms", published by the Phototype Company of Bombay and printed in Luxembourg, recreates the image of the lithographic postcard "A Fair Exchange"

Often financed by the East India Company, the early European photographers in India replaced not just the landscape and the portrait artists (Company School) but extended their role to support colonial designs through documentation and propaganda. Many of them were English army officers and surgeons living in India. The picture postcard started recording everything from 1910 onwards, not just the picturesque. The photographers took up ethnographic studies of the local population, capturing their everyday life, their religion and mythology. Famous personalities were photographed and photographic cataloguing of Indian antiquities was undertaken. The photographers travelled with the British Army, photographing the wars and the cantonment life with its club and sports facilities. They reported the news, were involved in land surveys and photographed the development of the railway network and other new technology or infrastructure and urban planning efforts undertaken in the large cities. Postcards featured the newly built town halls, high courts, universities, clubs, boulevards and gardens.

Images of the old modes of transport were one of the favourite subjects on early picture postcards, sent home by Europeans living in India. Horse-driven carriages (*ticca garhi*), *tonga*s, recklas, bullock carts, palanquins, camel and elephant rides continued as the favoured modes of personal transport for both Indians and Europeans. Hand-pulled rickshaws that first appeared in the hills of Simla around 1890 were introduced in Calcutta with much success. The British administration had initially turned the horse carriages into horse-driven trams in Bombay, Calcutta, Nasik and Patna. The electric tram was introduced in Madras in 1895 and, by 1910, in Bombay, Calcutta, Delhi and Kanpur. While a few rajas, Parsi merchants and English elite living in India did start importing the earliest cars (e.g., Oldsmobile) between 1901–1903, even by 1910, the cities of Bombay and Calcutta only had approximately 1,000 cars each. The commercialisation of motorcars in Europe and the US immediately after WWI did not quite translate to a parallel creation of a car industry in India. Relying on imports, it is estimated that by 1930 there were no more than 30,000 cars all across India.

Today, anyone working on the social history of that time can find an ocean of information in these picture postcards. There are even picture postcards about postcards, post offices and their processes, of stamps, coins and flags of that time. Often, postcards were used as a medium of commercial advertising, or as invitation for events or by shops and establishments to reach out to customers.

ABOVE:
Postcard titled
"The Rickshaw, Mussoorie"

ABOVE LEFT:
Postcard titled
"A Mussoorie Dandie"

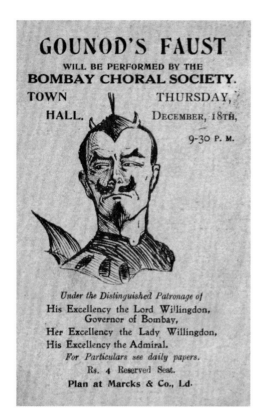

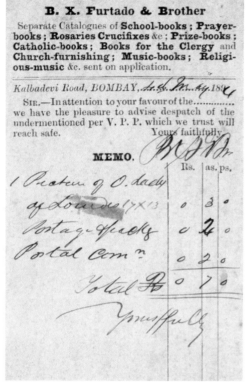

RIGHT:

A postcard used as an invitation card, in 1913, for a Faust performance in Bombay

EXTREME RIGHT:

A postcard used as a memo, in 1894, by Bombay-based B.X. Furtado & Brother

The colonial perspective comes out most clearly in the ethnographic subjects of the picture postcards which documented, at times mockingly, the "types of native people" of India and their "jobs or occupations". Coupled with books like *Behind my Bungalow* and *Inside the Katchery*, the lavish lifestyle of the colonial European with an army of servants became a popular subject of picture postcards sent back home by the Europeans. The text on the pictures often detailed the task ("*Chhota Hazri*" for breakfast), with a distinction made between the butler, the *khansamah*, the *khidmatgor* and the *bawarchi*. Many years later, the granddaughter of Babu Jagjivan Ram, a Dalit leader and freedom fighter of India, came across such postcards being sold on the streets of London, when she relocated there for her studies. Devangana Kumar, who grew up in elite Delhi bungalows as a politician's daughter, was so taken aback by the social inequalities of colonial India that she brought some of these picture postcards to India and created an exhibition showcasing them in

Native Waiter

248   Chota Hazri (Breakfast).

KHIDMATGOR.
(TABLE BOY.)

THE BUTLER.

BAWARCHI. (COOK.)

2012. Today, these picture postcards are an important reminder of India's past and not mere nostalgia of a time gone by.

From the time of the origin of postcards in the 1860s to the Golden Era of picture postcards until 1918, the usage of the term "India" was not completely settled. As Europeans had started carving out their part of the India/Indies/East-Indies with labels like Dutch Indies, Portuguese India, French India and British India, the stamps of the era defined these terms more clearly than the picture postcard labels. It is not unusual, therefore, to find India/l'Inde/Indien labelled postcards featuring picturesque Cambodia, Indonesia, Thailand and Vietnam.

History of the Picture Postcard—In India and Across the World

The immediate predecessor of picture postcards and one of the most significant landmarks in its evolution was the introduction of the "Correspondence Card", i.e. postcards without a picture, in 1869 in Austria-Hungary. This was based on the suggestion of Dr Emanuel Hermann in an article that he had written for the *Neue Freie Presse* newspaper. In its first avatar, the postcard was yellowish, measuring 122 x 85 mm, with one side exclusively for the address and the other side left blank for open communication. This correspondence card was immediately accepted by the European population and, in 1870, was introduced in England and several other countries. However, its introduction into British India and in many of the

FACING PAGE
Above Left:
Postcard titled "A Native Waiter"
Above Centre:
Postcard titled "Chota Hazri (Breakfast)"
Above Right:
Postcard titled "Khidmatgor (Table Boy)"
Below Left:
Postcard titled "The Butler"
Below Centre:
Postcard titled "Bawarchi (Cook)"
Below Right:
Postcard titled "A Khansamah (Cook)"

BELOW RIGHT:
A Portugese India correpondence card posted in 1900

BELOW:
A British East India correspondence card posted in 1898

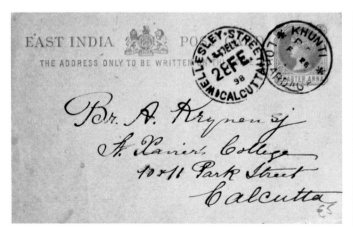

Indian princely states was not as smooth. Even though in 1878 the Universal Postal Union had introduced the postcard as a compulsory product on its list and had standardised the tariff rates for their circulation, it was only in July 1879 that British India launched its first postcard.

It is interesting to note that when Dr Hermann passed away the *New York Times* obituary in the 2 August 1903 issue had this to say about how his innovation was introduced in India:

> Somewhat amusing are the means by which the use of the postcard has been forced upon reluctant Governments, that of British India, for instance. Europeans in India, accustomed to the convenience of the postcard at home, clamored for a similar convenience in the East, but the Indian Post Office met their petitions, time after time, with the same answer. If postcards were issued no one would use them. The obvious retort, "Then why do so many people ask for them?" had no weight on the obdurate Post Office, and so matters went on till 1877, when a certain military officer became determined to prove that the Indian public would avail itself of the use of postcards were they able to do so.
>
> And so he issued a card bearing on the correspondence side his name and rank — "Frederick Brine, Lieutenant Colonel - Royal Engineers," and on these cards he conducted so much of his own correspondence as could he conduct on a card, and induced his friends to do the same, of course, affixing to the cards stamps to defray the current rate of postage for an ordinary letter. Numbers of these card-letters passed through the mail, and, annoyed at the object lesson taught to it, the Indian Post Office directed Colonel Brine to discontinue issuing them.
>
> The Colonel replied that if he and his friends chose to write their letters on pieces of cardboard, instead of sheets of paper, they would continue to do so, and that the Post Office could not compel the enclosing of a letter in an

THE LATE GENERAL F. BRINE, R.E.

This distinguished officer, who died in London on May 30, was the son of Major Brine, of the 7th Royal Fusiliers, and was born in June 1829. He served as a Volunteer in the Crimean campaign, at the siege of Sebastopol and the battle of the Tchernaya. He was also present in the flag-ship Euryalus at the naval engagement, under Vice-Admiral Kuper, off Japan, including the attacks on the shore batteries, in August 1863. For his services in the Chinese engagements he was thanked in despatches, breveted Major, and created a Knight of the Tower and Sword of Portugal. General Brine was one of the pioneers of the Volunteer movement in the British settlements in China. In 1867 he went to India, and was posted to the Public Works Department in the Punjaub. While in India he did much to improve the condition of the poorer class of Europeans, and introduced some useful measures in the postal service. After his retirement from the Army, with the honorary rank of Major-General, in 1884, he identified himself with ballooning. One of his adventures in attempting to cross over to France, when he was picked up in the Channel, will not have been forgotten.

The Portrait is from a photograph by Messrs. Maull and Young, Piccadilly.

THE LATE GENERAL FREDERICK BRINE, R.E.

ABOVE:

Portrait of Colonel Frederick Brine

ABOVE RIGHT:

Obituary of Colonel Brine that appeared in the Illustrated London News

envelope! The legal advisers to the Post Office held that he was right, and the Indian Government had to admit that, as a number of persons had found it convenient to conduct their correspondence on cards, though by doing so they saved nothing in postage, still greater numbers would use postcards which would pass through the post at half the ordinary letter rate. And so the gallant Colonel won his victory.

Upon Frederick Brine's death in May 1890, the 14 June 1890 issue of *The Illustrated London News* published a tribute to the late officer, recognising his achievements in the army and the changes he brought about in the postal services.

With skepticism and delay, when the Post Office of India finally introduced the correspondence card in July 1879, it priced the product at a mere quarter anna (a coinage type in India where 4 annas was the equivalent of one pie/pice/paise) for a delivery anywhere across the vast geography of British India. The product proved to be a huge success with the local population within India; by 1883, the Post Office had recorded an annual sale of 26 million postcards within the country.

In 1947, apart from the European colonies of the French and the Portuguese (the Danish and Dutch had moved out earlier), there were 562 princely or native states of India. At least 25 of these had their own postal departments which issued their respective postcards. The following Indian princely states are known to have issued postcards — Bamra, Barwani, Bhopal, Chamba, Charkhari, Cochin, Dhar, Duttia, Faridkot, Gwalior, Hyderabad, Indore, Jaipur, Jind, Kashmir, Kishangarh, Morvi, Nabha, Patiala, Rajasthan, Rajkot, Sirmor, Saurashtra, Travancore and Travancore-Cochin.

A few years later, some commercial establishments started advertising their products on one side of the postcard by introducing a monochrome picture of their product along with some text. One cannot really be certain but as it appears from postally used specimens that have come up in exhibitions and auctions, picture postcards were first introduced in India in 1896. In the first few years, they were quite expensive, largely imported by the British Indian Government or by private enterprises from publishers abroad and sold through bookshops frequented by Europeans living in India or at tourist spots. Over time, they began to be produced privately in India. None of the states issued picture postcards and hence the state-run post offices were never a point of sale of early picture postcards. So initially, this product that became very popular with the Europeans remained unaffordable for most of the local population, who continued using correspondence cards. Amongst the first Indians to use the early picture postcards of India, during the Golden Era, were the wealthy Parsis and Gujaratis of Bombay and the Marwari traders of Calcutta. Across Europe, correspondence cards were part of the state's post office stationery, and picture postcards originated through private production and enterprise in the 1870s. Several initiatives are documented, more prominent among them being those of the English book-printer Baron Raphael Tuck, who took to printing landscape paintings on his early postcards, and J. Miesler, the famous lithographer of Berlin.

Concurrent to the early years of the picture postcard in Europe (1870 to 1896) was the development of a photograph from a camera image, evolving from its inception in 1835 by Louis Daguerre to the time that George Eastman introduced his first Kodak camera in 1888. While many of the picture postcards during these initial years were cheaper lithographed pictures, some explorer photographers started printing photographs as postcards too. Photographic postcards of the Orient became a much-coveted item in Europe during the early years, even though most countries in the Orient had themselves not yet introduced the picture postcard. Over time, the drop in production prices of postcards was closely linked to the commercialisation of photography. Between 1860 and 1890, the camera was an expensive product and private photography explorers from Europe primarily sold images to newspapers and book/print publishers. These photography explorers basically followed the footprints of the painter-travellers such as Hodges, the Daniells and Forbes, as seen earlier in this chapter. Until the photography camera price reduced to make it a personal product in the 1890s, there were rapid advancements in picture printing technologies every few years. The commercial benefits of producing pictures of faraway places was the prime motivaton.

Picture postcards showing Indian subjects and landscapes were being produced in Austria, Germany, Luxembourg and England during the 1870s and 1880s. Amongst the earliest were the Austrian and German lithographed series with the "Gruss aus" or "Greetings From" title. While "Greetings from…" European countries and towns formed the bulk of such picture postcards, a few postcards titled "Gruss aus Indien" were printed in Germany and Austria. However, no one can really identify whether the "Gruss aus Indien" picture postcards were the first ones on the subject of India or not. There were some other early lithographed picture postcards with Indian subjects being used within Europe. One example of this is the classic "Tiger hunt on Elephant back" picture, titled "Indien", issued by Dess Company. The fascination for hunting tigers and cheetahs in the wild on elephant back continued to dominate postcard themes both in lithography and photography.

ABOVE:
Postcard titled "Indien"

LEFT:
*Postcard depicting a
tiger hunt*

H. M. King George Tiger shooting in India.

ABOVE:

*An Antoine Druet postcard
depicting a tiger hunt*

RIGHT:

*Postcard titled
"H.M. King George
Tiger Shooting in India"*

Introduction

29

A Hunting Cheeta.

Within Europe, one can also find some postcards from the year 1898 titled "Gruss aus Carl Hagenbeck's Indien" and many titled "J & G Hagenbeck's India" between 1898 and 1902 that had been issued from Germany and Czech Republic in German language (Gruss aus) and Czech language (Pozdrav od) respectively. These postcards showed scenes of India, particularly southern India, captured through high-quality early photography.

Carl Hagenbeck was a wealthy German businessman who imported animals from Africa, Ceylon and India, and was the first person to make commercial zoos in Europe and America. He was one of the first to conceptualise spectacular exhibitions featuring both animals and people in circus-like carnivals. In 1884, for instance, he had launched a successful Ceylon Exhibition showcasing 64 performers and 25 elephants. Millions of Europeans came to see this exhibition, including the Austrian King Franz Joseph II in Vienna, as it moved from Paris to London to Berlin. Following this success, he launched a bigger "India Exhibition"

ABOVE:

Postcard titled "Gruss aus Carl Hagenbeck's Indien 1898: Indisches Cafehaus" (Greetings from Carl Hagenbeck's India 1998: Indian Coffee House), posted in 1898 from Berlin to Mannheim, Germany

ABOVE RIGHT:

Postcard titled "J & G. Hagenbeck's Malabaren, Indien"

in 1898, creating an amusement park with large temporary Indian structures. Maharram Platz, Indischen Cafehaus and Trischinapoli Platz were the themes showcased by him in the busy Kurfurstendamm area of Berlin. The India Exhibition used picture postcards as an advertising tool. Carl Hagenbeck's half-brothers, John and Gustav, had organised the promotion. After the exhibition closed, these Hagenbeck postcards, marked with the "J & G Hagenbeck" signature, remained as popular early images of the exotic Orient and were sold for several years after that within Europe.

As production of picture postcards began in India itself and imports reduced, the subjects of these early India-made picture postcards reflected the British and European social life in India. A diverse array of subjects have been represented in postcards, particularly during the Golden Era, thus reflecting the popularity of the medium. The Europeans and the elite Indians sent these pictures in large numbers to family and friends abroad, sharing the visuals captured by the early photographers in India.

Another landmark event in the postal history of the world is the first official mail to be flown by a plane, the airmail, which was in India on 18 February 1911. This was an extension of an event organised by British aviation pioneer Walter Windham, when for the first time airplanes flew in Indian skies. The chaplain of the Holy Trinity Church at Allahabad requested the Indian Postal Department and Henri Pequet, a French pilot participating in the event, to undertake a short 7-mile journey from the Allahabad polo field to Naini to drop the mail, as a fundraising activity for a youth hostel. All letters and postcards on this flight were stamped with a mark and date of the event, making them popular collectibles to this day.

Speaking of postally used postcards, the earliest picture postcards posted from India in 1896 were the "Gruss aus" type, imported from Germany and Austria. Werner Roessler's "Gruss aus Indien" imports from Germany and Calcutta-based publisher D. Macropolo's "Greetings from India" and "Greetings from Calcutta" imported from Italy are some of the early picture postcards postally used in India. One of the earliest photo studios of Madras, Wiele and Klein, started by German photographers of the same name, had their postcards printed in Saxony in the similar "Greetings from South India" format.

Postcard titled "Greetings from India", posted in 1899 from Calcutta to Vienna through Sea Post

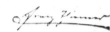

Souvenir of East Indies.

ABOVE:

Postcard titled "Souvenir of East Indies: Indische Schauspieler [Indian Actors]", posted in 1898 from Bombay to Planany, Czech Republic

ABOVE RIGHT:

Postcard titled "Souvenir of East Indies: Elefanten des Nizam von Hyderabad [Elephants of the Nizam of Hyderabad]", posted in 1899 from Hyderabad to Planany, Czech Republic

Another of the early postcard series, which was extensively in use between 1896 and 1904 in India was the "Weltreise" or "Voyage around the World" series published in Dresden. Picture postcards exclusively published for India and Burma, using early photographs (often hand-coloured), in this Voyage around the World series were titled "Souvenir of East Indies" in English. Most of these picture postcards which had been postally used in India and Burma had a stamp of "Army Zimmer" (Army Room, in German) on them. It appears that the European soldiers based in the cantonments of India and Burma may have been the first users of these picture postcards. The culture of innovation which was initiated by the efforts of Lieutenant Colonel Fredrick Brine with the British India Post Office seem to have been alive with the European soldiers some fifteen years later.

Picture Postcard Genres and Collections

Apart from the categorisation of postcards by their production techniques, be it lithography (stone-printing planographic technique) or phototyping (photography) or by their vintage (Golden Era), one other key categorisation of picture postcards is based on the World Postal Agreement of member countries in the year 1906. With this agreement, the back of the picture postcards was to be divided vertically into two equal halves—the left half to write the address and the right half to write a message. Britain had already initiated these divided-back picture postcards in 1902. By 1907, all countries switched, including India Post. The picture postcards prior to this agreement were known as undivided-back postcards since the entire reverse side of the postcard contained the address and the front a picture. At best, one could scribble a message below the picture on such postcards.

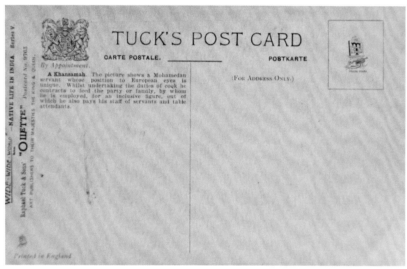

ABOVE:
A divided-back postcard issued by Raphael Tuck & Sons

LEFT:
An undivided-back British India postcard issued by the Universal Postal Union

A 4-fold panorama postcard of Bombay, 1905

Between 1905 and 1918, another innovation in postcards was the introduction of multiple-fold panoramas. Such long panoramas of European towns became a popular collectible and though relatively heavy in weight, these panorama postcards were often not inserted in envelopes but posted with stamps and address written on one side. Each fold always adhered to the standard postcard size of 5.8 x 4.1 inches. Some specimens of long panorama postcards, ranging from 2 to 8 folds and even upto 16 folds, for example, the panorama of Constantinople/Istanbul, have been found. Some Asian cities, too, feature in these multiple-fold panorama postcards. After many years of being on the lookout, we finally did come across an India panorama. This is a 4-fold panorama of Bombay bearing the title "Bombay - Panoramic view of Fort and Harbour from Clock Tower - Esplanade Hotel, Sailor's Home and Harbour from Clock Tower". Published by the Phototype Company, Bombay, the postcard had been postally used on 22 July 1905 by a German visiting Bombay and writing back home. Since there is no trace of a postal stamp on it, it appears to have been sent in an envelope to Germany.

Any type of art form could be depicted on postcards, be it cartoons, maps, paintings, lithographic/aquatint/etching prints, photographs and even embroidery. Innovations like 3-D postcards, pop-up cards and perfumed cards were experimented with as well.

Collecting postcards became a popular hobby as production prices dropped, postage stamps became standardised (starting with the UK Postal Service in

1840), and international postal unions collaborated to create a smooth global network. The Universal Postal Union commenced with a treaty in Switzerland in October 1874. Fan clubs opened in various parts of the world and exchanging postcards became a popular hobby, second only to philately.

Today, as the internet world moves personal photos to digital storage and online curation, the history of the "photo album" is almost forgotten. In the pre-photography era, getting a personal or family painting done was the luxury of the elite—the kings, nobles and the wealthy. With the advent of the camera, personal photographs in the form of "Carte de Viste" became popular in the 1850s and 1860s. Those who could afford it went to a studio and had a personal or family picture taken. These would be shared through a display book at home. When the picture postcard came in, the affordability and craze during the Golden Era is what gave birth to the photo album. The photo album in the corner of a drawing room became the pride of families. Collecting picture postcards showing different parts of the world became a household hobby in Europe.

Photo Albums of Mahabaleshwar, Nainital, Mt. Abu and Bijapur put together by local studios. Prominent booksellers like Thacker & Co., and publishers like H.A Mirza & Sons also compiled postcards of Bombay and Delhi into albums for sale through their commercial outlets

As the production prices of photographs reduced, the picture postcards in the photo albums were replaced by personal photographs of travels to different lands. The period between 1920 and 1935 is particularly interesting because the photo albums from this period are typically a mix of personal photographs taken during the travels and picture postcards of that region. In keeping with the times, several photography studios offered a photo production in the exact size of a standard picture postcard and with a divided back on the reverse, creating a "personalised picture postcard" that could immediately be posted from a nearby post office, during the travels itself. These personalised picture postcards, though, did not print the header "Gruss aus" or "Greetings from", a style of picture postcards that had already become the "old-style" by the 1920s.

INDIA TRAVEL AND TRANSPORTATION (1890–1947)

Around 1800 CE, the strength of the horse was the measure of speed and mobility. As technology-lead mass travel began with the invention of the railway in Europe, so did the romance of travel. Beginning with Switzerland and its neighbourhood of

Austria and Germany, came a novelty that gained popularity circa 1840: "Vedute", a series of etchings and engraving prints of picturesque views and prospects showing famous mountains, lakes, churches and castles, to be taken home as collectible souvenirs from holidays. These were the forerunners of the picture postcards. The technology of cheaper printing through steel engravings and then photographic productions was concurrent to the technological innovations in mass travel. In 1873, Jules Verne's famous novel *Around the World in Eighty Days* defined the timelines for the shortest travel around the world with a mix of high-speed trains, coaches and travel by ships. By 1890, such travels and low-cost printing both became mass products. New rail lines between 1860 and 1930s and new roads for the new inventions of cars and buses between 1910 and 1940s laid the foundation for the widespread land travel which we take for granted today. Picture postcards of that time provide a rare peep into that pioneering phase of mankind.

Travel to India—By Sea and Air

The key factor which facilitated travel to India was the opening of the Suez Canal in November 1869, the same year that Dr Emanuel Hermann conceptualised the postcard. By 1890, several shipping lines offered choices to arrive at 5 ports in India and Ceylon—Karachi, Bombay, Madras, Calcutta and Colombo. The sea voyage from Europe to India had reduced to less than 3 weeks by the turn of the century. The fabled "Sea Route to India" marked in European cartography for 400 years had new markers on the journey through the Suez to include the ports of Trieste and Brindisi in Italy, Marseilles in France and Aden in Egypt.

The international post also moved along the same sea route during this period. Stamps on the postcards reflect this route with fascinating postal marks of "Via Brindisi", "Via Trieste", etc., stamped enroute their journey from Indian towns to European addresses.

In 1927, Britain's Imperial Airways extended its passenger operations across the Empire with a De Havilland Hercules flight on the Cairo (Egypt)–Basra (Iraq)–Karachi–Jodhpur–Delhi route. A young JRD Tata launched India's

H. H. The Khedive Ismail and F. de Lesseps opening the Suez Canal in 1869.

ABOVE:

Postcard titled "H.H. The Khedive Ismail and F. De Lesseps opening the Suez Canal in 1869", published in Port Said

RIGHT:

Postcard titled "Bird's Eye View of the Suez Canal", published in Port Said

first commercial airline in 1932 and personally flew a single-engine aircraft from Karachi to Bombay via Ahmedabad. The airline, however, largely relied on ferrying Indian post (airmail) for its commercial viability. In its initial years, the annual passengers using these flights totaled to just over two hundred. By the time WWII began in 1938, KLM, Imperial Airways and Air France had all initiated weekly flights from Europe to India. However, passenger volumes were very low for these expensive air services and big shipping lines continued to ferry the bulk of international travellers to India. It is only with safer skies at the end of WWII in 1945 that commercial airlines started to provide real alternatives to the ship route through the Suez. But by 1947, even the Karachi to Bombay flight had become an international journey, while the flight from Karachi to Dacca was a national one, but for a new country, not India.

Travel in India—Exploring the Railway Routes

Between 1890–1947, the key factor facilitating travel within India was the spread of the railway network, which, over time, had connected all parts of the country. In 1909, one could break their journey and Indian Railways allowed the traveller to spend 16 days on this journey with one through ticket.

The primary motivation of the East India Company to introduce railways to India in 1849 was an economic and political one. The traditional movement of goods across India was on rivers and through waterways. Having captured the key sea ports of Calcutta, Madras and Bombay, the movement of commodities like cotton, spices and tea from the agricultural fields of mainland India to these ports often involved signing up treaties for rights on the river ports as well, for example, the development of Kanpur on the Ganga as the conduit port between Lucknow/Awadh on the Gomti River and Calcutta/East India Company on Ganga/Bengal bay. The railways offered a faster and more efficient movement of goods to the ports, at least within the territories of the 3 East India Company presidencies (Bombay, Calcutta and Madras). The other motivation was the expansion of the Company's territories through war. The British East India Company had already suffered heavy casualties and a defeat in the first Anglo-Afghan war (1839–1842).

For faster movement of troops, ammunition and weapons to the North-West Frontier Province (NWFP) and other areas of conflict, from their port hubs, the railways offered a solution. However, the money to finance such a venture in India, and to bring in technology from England was a challenge for the East India Company.

Riding on the back of success of the private enterprise in commercialising the new technology of steam engines and railways in England, R.M. Stephenson and a few other businessmen set up the East Indian Railway (EIR) Company. They signed a contract with the East India Company on 17 August 1849, entitling them to construct and operate a 100-mile railway line between Calcutta and Rajmahal in the Bengal Presidency, with the potential to extend it to Delhi via Mirzapur. On the same day, the East India Company signed a contract with another company in Bombay, the Great Indian Peninsula Railway (GIPR) Company, to construct and operate an experimental line of 35 miles between Bombay and Kalyan in the Bombay Presidency, which would later be extended to connect Khandesh (Malwa, modern-day western Madhya Pradesh) and Berar (modern-day eastern Madhya Pradesh) states, and onwards to the Calcutta and Madras Presidencies. EIC signed a contract with the Madras Railway Company in 1852 to construct a 70-mile railway line between Madras and Arcot with a provision to extend branches to Bombay, Calcutta, Deccan, Bangalore and the foot of the Nilgiris.

The first railway line in India, between Bombay and Thane (a distance of 21 miles) had opened for public use as early as 16 April 1853. The GIPR extended the line to Kalyan in May 1854 and further to Khopoli via Palasdhari by 1858. But crossing over the Western Ghats presented one of the biggest challenges ever for the Indian Railways—it took 5 years of engineering effort at a cost of half a million pound sterling and the loss of lives of several Indian workers to negotiate the tough 13-km stretch of crossing the Bhore Ghat. High embankments, nearly 2.5 km of tunneling and 8 viaducts were built. The subsequent line onwards to Pune and beyond continued to be developed in parallel. The challenge of Bhore Ghat is captured well by early photographers, including Samuel Bourne, and

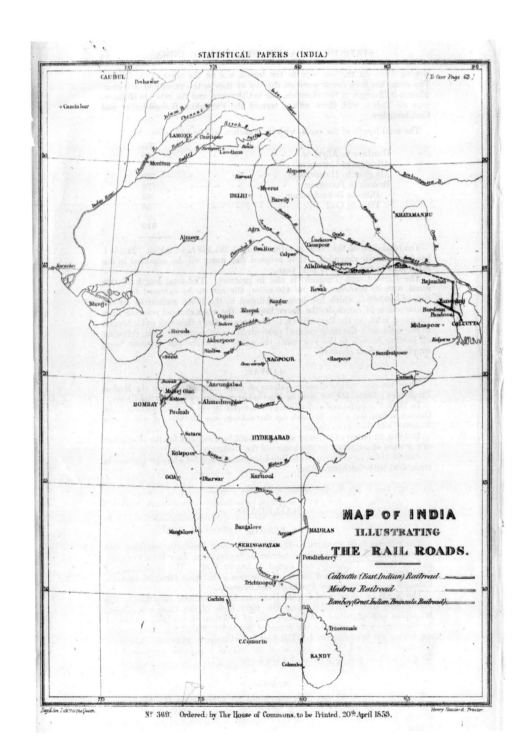

[To face Page 63.]

MAP OF INDIA
ILLUSTRATING
THE RAIL ROADS.

Calcutta (East Indian) Railroad _____
Madras Railroad _____
Bombay (Great Indian Peninsula Railroad) _____

Day & Son, Lith.rs to the Queen.

Nº 369.   Ordered, by The House of Commons, to be Printed, 20th April 1853.

Henry Hansard, Printer.

Map of India Illustrating the Rail Roads, ordered by the House of Commons, 20 April 1853. This map highlights the first railway routes in the Bombay, Bengal and Madras presidencies. It was commissioned just four days after the inauguration of India's first passenger rail service on the GIPR line between Bombay and Thane many postcards, even 50 to 70 years later, feature photographs of the railway line commemorating the engineering feat.

The liberal terms of the contracts offered by the East India Company to these pioneering companies in the presidencies—namely the East Indian Railway (Calcutta, 1849), the Great Indian Peninsula Railway (Bombay, 1849) and the Madras Guaranteed Railway (Madras, 1852)—practically assured attractive returns on investment to the shareholders. Upon the success of this model, the East India Company entered into 5 more "Guaranteed" return contracts— Bombay, Baroda and Central India Railway (BB&CI) in 1855, the Sind Railway (Sind, Punjab and Delhi) in 1856, the Eastern Bengal Railway in 1858, the Great Southern of India Railway (later merged with Carnatic Railway to form the South Indian Railway) in 1858, and Calcutta and South-Eastern Railway in 1859.

Interestingly, the East India Company guaranteed a 5 per cent return on investment in these 8 companies for an unlimited time period (even 25 years was not deemed acceptable) to the promoters. After the First War of Indian Independence in 1857, the Crown took over as the Government of India from the Company. Just for the period 1858 to 1900, the government paid GBP 51.5 million from the revenues, as dividend payments against the guaranteed railway contracts to these private English companies. On top of it, 1858 onwards, the cost of managing railways in India, such as wages of European workers in India and pensions for any European who had ever served in India, etc., was also included in the dubious "Home Charges" paid by the Government of India to England, often in the form of gold bullion sent by the shipload.

By 1869, the financial drain on Government of India because of these guaranteed returns to the private railway companies was all too obvious and the then viceroy, Lord Lawrence, famously made a statement that "whole profits go to the Companies, and the whole loss to the Government". Finally, in 1879, the state (GOI) purchased the first of the old guaranteed railways, the EIR, for a sum of GBP 32.75 million, which was to be paid in annuities of GBP 1.47 million from

January 1880 to February 1953. While the government took charge of the earliest eight guaranteed railway companies, it continued the practice of contracting private companies for most of the new expansion lines, but now under GOI finance and without guarantees. Punjab Northern, Rajputana–Malwa, Northern Bengal, Tirhoot, and Rangoon and Irrawady Railways came up during this phase. Many of the princely states also introduced railways in their respective territories and were encouraged by the GOI to integrate with their network of state-owned and private companies. Baroda state laid a line in 1873 and was followed by Hyderabad, Morvi, Bhavnagar, Gondal, Porbander, Jodhpur, Bhopal, Patiala, Junagad, Kashmir, Kolhapur, Rajkot, Jetpur, Mysore, Bikaner, Cooch Behar, Gwalior, Mewar, Kota, Jamnagar, Rajpipla, Dhrangadhra, Parlakimedi, Cambay, Malerkotla, Jind, Cochin, Travancore, Cutch, Jaipur, Mayurbhanj, Sangli, Dholpur and, finally, Bhawalpur in 1911.

By 1936, there were approximately 25 different railway systems in India, covering a distance of 42,000 miles in total. Just four of these 25 were state controlled, managing 18,500 miles of railway journeys. Out of these, the North-Western Railway served the Punjab, NWFP and Sind; the Great Indian Peninsula Railway served the Deccan, Bombay, Central Provinces and the Western United Provinces; the East Indian Railway served Bengal, Eastern United Provinces and Bihar; and, finally, the Eastern Bengal Railway served the area around the Brahmaputra River. To control and supervise the vast expanse of the Indian Railway with its different entities, a Railway Board was set up. Initially, this was part of the PWD (Public Works Department) of the GOI, but subsequently it was made subordinate to the Ministry of Commerce and Industries for better financial control.

The economic focus of the British Indian government was very clear in how it managed the Indian Railways. The government in England anyway charged a management fee from the British Indian government (which it controlled and made key appointments in) as part of the "Home Charges" levied. This conflict-of-interest position, leading to a deliberate drain on the Indian economy to better the

English economy was highlighted by Dadabhai Naoroji in his work *Poverty and Un-British Rule in India*, and by R.C. Dutt in his work *The Economic History of India in the Victorian Age*. The contracts, management costs and expansion of Indian Railways came at a huge economic cost to India. The Home Charges accounting turned around the export-import imbalance from a situation favouring India (due to the large export of commodities like cotton, spices, etc.) into one favouring England. In 1853, Karl Marx had forewarned of just this adverse impact of the railways on the economy of India. Mahatma Gandhi too was extremely critical of the railways. In 1909, he wrote in the *Hind Swaraj*:

> …But for the railways, the English could not have such a hold on India as they have. …Railways have also increased the frequency of famines, because, owing to facility of means of locomotion, people sell out their grain, and it is sent to the dearest markets. People become careless, and so the pressure of famine increases. Railways accentuate the evil nature of man: Bad men fulfil their evil designs with greater rapidity. The holy places of India have become unholy. Formerly, people went to these places with very great difficulty. Generally, therefore, only the real devotees visited such places. Nowadays rogues visit them in order to practice their roguery.

Besides the economic and political impact of the railways in India, the social impact, which Mahatma Gandhi was concerned with, was felt globally wherever the railways was introduced. Wolfgang Schivelbusch, a German cultural historian, sums it up in his 1977 book *The Railway Journey*:

> The railroad, the destroyer of experiential time and space, thus also destroyed the educational experience of the Grand Tour. Henceforth, the localities were no longer spatially individual or autonomous: they were points in the circulation of traffic that made them accessible. As we have seen, that traffic was the physical manifestation of the circulation of goods. From that time on, the places visited by the traveler became increasingly similar to the commodities that were part of the same circulation system. For the

twentieth-century tourist, the world has become one huge department store of countrysides and cities.

The industrialisation of travel which commenced with the railways, continued with the airways, as speed of travel became the focus. This kind of point-to-point travel tends to ignore the lay of the land. The travel guide book was born during this phase of the early railways. Unlike the erstwhile travelogues, cities and sites became the focus of these guide books, where travel writers described their routes, as much as the sites themselves. Some of the earliest guide books on India were written by H.G. Keane. Other pioneers of the travel guide books were Karl Baedeker of Germany, and John Murray and Thomas Cook of England. These guide books simplified and standardised the travel experience with a focus on describing sites, hotels and transportation facilities at the points of arrival and departure, i.e. at the ports and railway stations. The shipping and railway companies chose these points or the cities and towns. The government chose the companies and often financed and owned them. During the colonial days, the focus was clearly economic and political. While railways is a separate ministry by itself and the Railway Board of India no longer reports to the Ministry of Commerce and Industry, to this day, the Indian Railways makes more money through freight than passenger ticket sales.

Looking back, the years 1869 to 1871 became a turning point in Indian travel: (a) Opening of the Suez in 1869 brought the ports of India and Europe much closer (b) Calcutta and Bombay were connected by rail roads in 1870 (c) Lahore and Calcutta were connected via Mughal Sarai (U.P.) to Lahore route in 1870 (d) Bombay and Madras were connected by a rail link in 1871. All of this meant that by 1890, a European visitor with 4 months of time on his hands could arrive by ship to an Indian port and take well-planned tours covering Delhi, Calcutta, Lahore, Madras and Bombay by train, facilitated by travel companies like Thomas Cook & Co., and John Murray & Co.

Based on such travel guides and the rail and road routes used during the Golden Era of picture postcards in India, we have curated the picture postcards in this

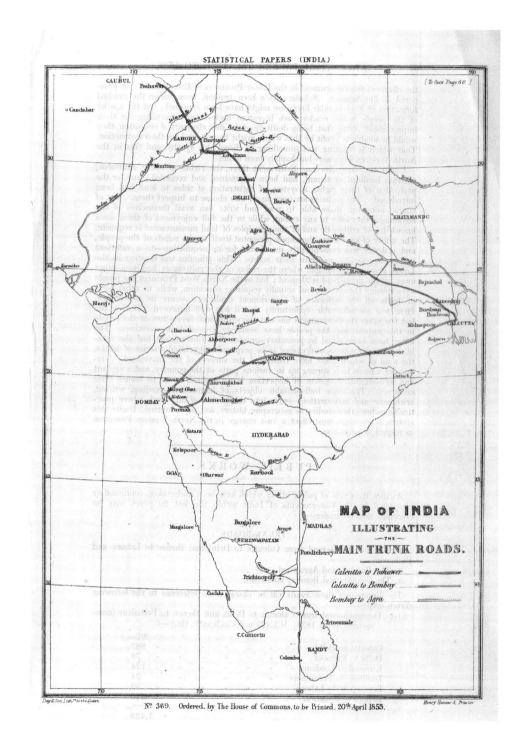

(To face Page 60.)

MAP OF INDIA
ILLUSTRATING
THE
MAIN TRUNK ROADS.

Calcutta to Peshawer
Calcutta to Bombay
Bombay to Agra

N° 369. Ordered, by The House of Commons, to be Printed, 20th April 1853.

Day & Son, Lith.rs to the Queen.

Henry Hansard, Printer.

Map of India Illustrating the Main Trunk Roads, ordered by the House of Commons, 20 April 1853. The map highlights the strategic road connections between Calcutta and Peshawar (via Delhi and Lahore), between Calcutta and Bombay (via Nagpur) and between Bombay and Agra

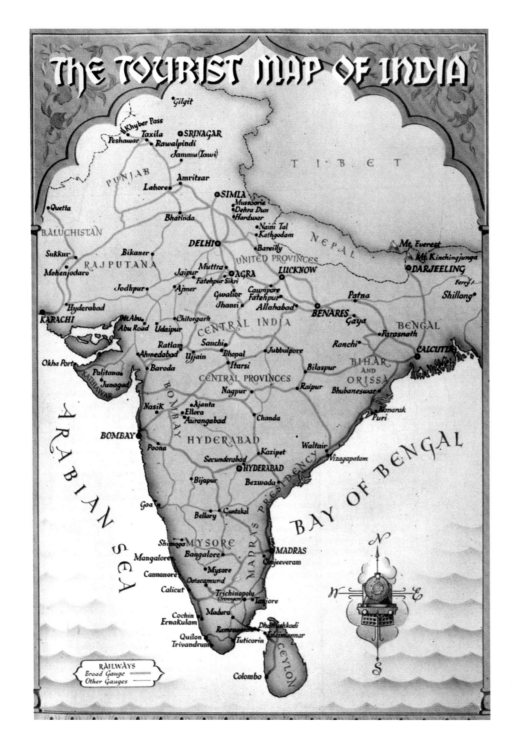

THE TOURIST MAP OF INDIA

A tourist map of India highlighting the provinces and railway routes published in The Handbook of India, *2nd edition, issued by The Central Publicity Bureau, Railway Board, Delhi, c. 1930*

book in a sequence, to showcase the visual experience of a traveller of that time. The postcards date right upto 1947, and our focus is on topographical views, and many important Indian towns only appear in picture postcards for the first time in the 1930s and 1940s. There are beautiful postcards of both Burma (Myanmar) and Ceylon (Sri Lanka) from the colonial years, however, our focus in this book is just India. The six chapters of the book and their titles reflect the big towns and the large states of India and Pakistan as they were a hundred years back:

1. North-West Frontier Province, Punjab (Lahore, Amritsar) and Delhi
2. Kashmir and United Provinces
3. Baluchistan, Sindh (Karachi), Rajputana and Gujarat (Kutch, Kathiawar)
4. Bombay, Goa and Central Provinces (Berar, Bastar)
5. Bengal (Calcutta), Darjeeling, Sikkim, Assam, Bihar and Orissa
6. Hyderabad, Mysore (Bangalore) and Madras (Pondicherry and Travancore)

The bunching of states in these chapter titles happened on its own as we searched road and rail routes in old travelogues and travel guides. The fissures of the partitioning of India and Pakistan in 1947 are quite apparent in the road and rail blocks created by new borders. The lay of the land, which the old routes (often ancient ones of the mystic "Silk Road") took into consideration, have been forgotten in the border areas today as defense considerations have taken over. But these old pictures can certainly fuel our imagination of a borderless world from the days of yore and make us forget the political realities of today. Sometimes that imagination can open new roads and remove walls. That, dear reader, is our hope.

The Mall Rawalpindi

NORTH-WEST FRONTIER PROVINCE

PUNJAB

&

DELHI

Postman

The northern states of India—The North-West Frontier Province (NWFP) and Punjab—were reeling from the impact of the Anglo-Sikh Wars, the two Anglo-Afghan wars, and preparing for a third during the early years of the picture postcards (1896 to 1918). In preparation of a strong defence in the region, an extensive railway and military road network was developed and large well-planned cantonments came up in Peshawar, Rawalpindi and Umballa (Ambala).

Field Telegraph Office

FACING PAGE:
Postcard titled "Postman"

RIGHT:
Postcard titled "Field Telegraph Office"

In the NWFP, the Khyber Pass, the fabled entry to India from Afghanistan through the Hindu Kush, had for years been under the strategic control of the Afridis, the dominant Pathan tribe in the region. Over time, these Pathans were enlisted in the Army under the Khaibar Corps of Rifles. The Tirah Field Force near the border with Afghanistan and the Mohmand Field Force controlling the Shabkadar Fort at the mouth of the pass were well known. The war photographers—Fred Bremner, Holmes and Mela Ram—were trained and financed by the EIC (East India Company) to photo-document this growth of military and administrative presence in this region. Many of their photos were released as postcards.

Interested travellers could obtain a permit for day trips from Peshawar up the narrow Khyber Pass right upto the Afghan border by road or by the Khyber Pass Railway, inaugurated in 1925. The photographers captured the rough mountainous scenery with walled towering villages and terraced fields being guarded by armed Pathans. On two days of the week, the Khyber Pass was open to the inflow of caravans from Central Asia and postcards show the two-way road filled with long strings of camels, men, women, children, droves of goat and sheep, with bales of merchandise, all guarded by large and fierce dogs.

The chief fortified posts along the way from Peshawar to the Khyber Pass were the Jamrud Fort at the entrance of the pass, Ali Masjid halfway through and Landi Kotal at the head of the Pass. The steep descent of 2,000 feet towards Landi Khana in Afghan territory lay just beyond. Till the early 1900s, the railway line came up to Jamrud only and the rest of the journey was made on *tonga*s. Summer trips to the hill cantonment of Cherat and to Khanspur near Abbottabad were quite popular and are captured in picture postcards.

The five administrative divisions of the Punjab province were Lahore, Rawalpindi, Mooltan (Multan), Jullundur (Jalandhar) and Delhi besides a number of princely states. One of the oldest and most famous roads of Asia, the Rah-e-Azam, ran through the NWFP and Punjab connecting Kabul to Calcutta. Rah-e-Azam passed through Peshawar, Delhi, Lucknow, Allahabad and Benares (Varanasi). Between

1833 and 1860, the EIC renovated this road and renamed it the Grand Trunk Road. By 1870, railway tracks were laid parallel to the road, offering a much faster movement of goods (arms, initially), people and troops. Picture postcards follow the journey of the newly laid North-Western or Punjab Railway that connected Peshawar with Lahore and Delhi, crossing the Indus at Attock over its famous fortified iron girder bridge. Further, the train passed through Rawalpindi and thereafter continued to Amritsar, Jullundur, Ludhiana, Sirhind, Rajpura, Umballa, Saharanpur, Sardhana, Meerut and Ghaziabad Junction, running along the eastern bank of the river Yamuna. The North-West Frontier was also connected to the central railway network through Mooltan and to Quetta through the Bolan Pass. Even before the railway network had come up in this region, Mooltan had been the collection depot for all trade within central Punjab. Goods reached the city down the Ravi and Jhelum Rivers and then onwards the Indus flotilla to the Karachi port for shipment to Europe. This connecting link of Mooltan with Sindh helped the British receive the first outside assistance during the revolt in Punjab.

Agra to Peshawar :

Aligarh ...	Dâk Bungalow	Excellent	Supplies
Delhi	Cecil Hotel	,,	—
Umballa ...	Robson's Hotel	Fair	—
Ludhiana ...	Dâk Bungalow	Excellent	Supplies
Lahore ...	Nedou's Hotel	Fair	—
,,	Charing Cross Hotel	Very poor	
Wazirabad ...	Dâk Bungalow	Poor *	Supplies
Gujarkhan ...	,,	Very poor	No supplies
Rawal Pindi ...	Flashman's Hotel	Good	—
Peshawar ...	Alexandra Hotel	Very good	—
Amritsar ...	Cambridge Hotel	Excellent	—

Hotels and dak bungalows en route Agra to Peshawar listed in the book Motoring in India: A Guide for the Tourist and Resident *by Charles Watney and Mrs Herbert Lloyd, published by Car Illustrated Ltd, London, 1909*

Lahore, the pride of the Mughal Empire, and where Ranjit Singh held his durbar at the Shish Mahal displaying the Koh-i-noor, was made the provincial capital of Punjab by the British upon annexation in 1849. Picture postcards of Lahore, which evolved as a centre of arts, culture and learning, capture the Mughal architecture and the new public buildings built by the British with guidance from John Lockwood Kipling and the engineer R.B. Gangaram.

Till the 1890s, the sacred city of Amritsar, as a commercial and industrial centre of Punjab, was wealthier and more populated than the cultural capital of Lahore. Like Peshawar, traders and merchants of various nationalities thronged the bazaars of Amritsar. The postcards capture the hustle-bustle of the bazaars and, on the other hand, also feature serene images of the Golden Temple reflecting in the surrounding tank, bordered by fruit gardens, palaces and residences of the wealthy nobles, the minars and towers, prominent among them being the Baba Atal tower, which had its inner walls painted with the life story of Guru Nanak.

Ferozepore, the "land of the martyrs", became a border town between India and Pakistan in 1947. The city has memorial parks of freedom fighters of India which feature prominently in picture postcards. Further on the North-Western Railway, after an hour's journey from Rajpura on a branch line, one reached Patiala, which had been the capital of the Sikh State in the late 1800s. Maharaja Rajendra Singh's richly decorated palace became an interesting subject of picture postcards.

The Amritsar-Pathankot Railway provided connections to Dalhousie, which was reached by hiring a *tonga* or pony or *dhooly* from Danera. From Dalhousie, Chamba lay across the river Ravi. A postcard in this series captures the general view of Khajjiar at the foothills of the Dhauladhar range in the Chamba district. Khajjiar is amongst the 160 locations recognised as bearing striking topographical resemblance to Switzerland. On reaching Pathankot, *tonga*s could be hired for the picturesque and steep ascent to Dharamshala, the headquarters of the Kangra district. The 1905 earthquake had a huge impact on the region, destroying several of its old temples. Photographers documented the impact, which subsequently featured in picture postcards of the region.

The "Simla Exodus" was the great Anglo-Indian event in the summer months, when the Viceroy and his entire administration shifted their offices to this summer capital in the hills. Postcards of Simla (Shimla) capture the growth of this hill station, with its humble beginnings after the end of the Gorkha wars (1815–16), when, in 1819, the first thatched wooden cottage of a British officer came up. In the late 19th century, Simla had grown to have more than a thousand built residences, several new government buildings, post offices, clubs, sports and other recreational facilities. Perhaps Kipling's stories further encouraged people to come up to Simla in summer and experience the excitement of being there for themselves.

To facilitate ease and enjoyment of travel to the hills, the Delhi–Umballa–Kalka broad gauge railway started in 1891, followed by the Kalka-Simla Railway, inaugurated by Lord Curzon in 1903. The 96-km long picturesque journey, which is now part of the Mountain Railways of India UNESCO World Heritage Sites, was captured extensively in postcards, along with glimpses from its construction phase. Mostly following the old Tonga Road, passing through Dharampur, Kumarhatti or Dagshai Cantonment, the journey took about seven hours on the way up and six hours on the return. There were 103 tunnels to go through, and the Barogh Tunnel at a height of 3,752 feet was at that time the longest tunnel in India. Engineer Colonel Barogh, after whom the tunnel is named, had supervised its digging from both ends, and when it didn't align was symbolically fined one rupee! Out of shame, he committed suicide inside the incomplete tunnel, which was later believed to have been completed with the blessings of a local sadhu!

Kasauli, another popular hill sanitarium, was reached from Kalka by the old Simla road or by rail to Dharampur and then by tonga up a steep road.

Chandigarh emerged as a well-planned city only after India's independence, and its topographical development is largely captured in later-day postcards. However, dating back to the Golden Era, we found rare postcards of the open undeveloped spaces of Chandigarh which were being used as a campsite for the moving army regiments.

Another rare pre-1907 postcard of this region is of the remote town of Wangtu, which is situated close to the Indo-China border on the old Hindustan-Tibet Road in the Kinnaur district of Himachal Pradesh. The picture postcard shows one of the largest wooden bridges of the Himalayan region, built over the swiftly flowing Sutlej River.

Delhi was transferred to the Punjab Province from the North-Western Province (later called the United Provinces) in 1859, following the First War of Independence of 1857. The forts, palaces, stepwells, temples, mosques and tombs, reminiscent of Delhi's seven ancient cities that stretched between the Ridge and the river Jumna (Yamuna), were extensively photographed and later printed as postcards. H.A. Mirza was one of the most prominent publishers of postcards of Delhi. Their postcards capture Shah Jahan's symbols of equality and justice, as reflected in "The Scales of Justice" at Red Fort's Diwan-i-Khas and the mural of Orpheus playing music to a group of animals in the Diwan-i-Am. Princess Jahanara Begum's Chandni Chowk with its jewellers of Dariba Kalan (*Dur-e-be-baha*, meaning "an incomparable pearl" in Persian), the attar and fabric sellers, the embroiderers and all other traditional artisans were carefully photo-documented. Postcards of Delhi also feature the newly built town hall, clock tower, library and banks in the old city.

With the shift of the Empire's capital from Calcutta to Delhi in 1911, postcards mark the events of the two Delhi Durbars (1903 and 1911). The making of the new capital, with its secretariat and administrative buildings, churches, hotels and residential quarters that came up with the increasing population of European residents, became a popular subject in picture postcards of Delhi. A rare and interesting postcard in this series advertises the "Imre Schwaiger's Art Museum" at Alipore Road, Civil Lines, located just across the Oberoi Maidens Hotel. Imre Schwaiger (1868–1940) was a well-known Hungarian art expert and collector living in Delhi. Under his guidance, the London-based jeweller Jacques Cartier had purchased several Mughal, Hindu, Jain and Buddhist objects d'art and jewels from antique collectors and traders of Delhi.

ENTRANCE OF KHYBER PASS.

TITLE:
Entrance of Khyber Pass

PRINTER/PUBLISHER:
Printed in Saxony

PHOTOGRAPHER/ARTIST:
Mela Ram Photographer, Peshawar

Khyber Pass.

TITLE:
Khyber Pass

TITLE:
Landi Kotal

PRINTER/PUBLISHER:
Printed in England

PHOTOGRAPHER/ARTIST:
Randolph Bezant Holmes, Peshawar

UNDIVIDED BACK

JAMROOD FORT.

TITLE:
Jamrood Fort

PRINTER/PUBLISHER:
Printed in Saxony

PHOTOGRAPHER/ARTIST:
Mela Ram Photographer, Peshawar

KHYBER PASS ON THE RETURN TO PESHAWAR FROM ALI MUSJID.

TITLE:
Khyber Pass on the Return to Peshawar from Ali Musjid

PRINTER/PUBLISHER:
Printed in Saxony

PHOTOGRAPHER/ARTIST:
Mela Ram Photographer, Peshawar

TIRAH FIELD FORCE.

TITLE:
Tirah Field Force

PRINTER/PUBLISHER:
Printed in Saxony

PHOTOGRAPHER/ARTIST:
Mela Ram Photographer, Peshawar

Shabkadar Fort (Mohmand Field Force)

GENL. WILLCOCKS' RESIDENCE AT SHABKADAR

TITLE:
*Shabkadar Fort
(Mohmand Field Force)*

PRINTER/PUBLISHER:
Printed in Saxony

PHOTOGRAPHER/ARTIST:
Baljee

GOD BLESS YOUR EXCELLENCIES

Kabli Gate, Peshawar

TITLE:
Kabli Gate, Peshawar

PRINTER/PUBLISHER:
*H.A. Mirza & Sons, Delhi;
printed in Germany*

VICTORIA MEMORIAL HALL, PESHAWAR.

TITLE:
Victoria Memorial Hall, Peshawar

PRINTER/PUBLISHER:
Printed in Saxony

PHOTOGRAPHER/ARTIST:
Mela Ram Photographer, Peshawar

RESIDENCY HOUSE.

TITLE:
Residency House

PRINTER/PUBLISHER:
Printed in Saxony

PHOTOGRAPHER/ARTIST:
Mela Ram Photographer, Peshawar

CAMEL MARKET, PESHAWAR.

TITLE:
Camel Market, Peshawar

PRINTER/PUBLISHER:
Printed in Saxony

PHOTOGRAPHER/ARTIST:
Mela Ram Photographer, Peshawar

Khans pur.

TITLE:
Khans Pur

PRINTER/PUBLISHER:
H.A. Mirza & Sons, Delhi;
printed in Germany

Afreedi House.

TITLE:
Afreedi House

The Bazaar — Cherat Hill.

TITLE:
The Bazaar - Cherat Hill
PRINTER/PUBLISHER:
Moorli Dhur & Sons, Ambala;
printed in Germany

TITLE:
Cherat Badges

PRINTER/PUBLISHER:
Printed in Saxony

PHOTOGRAPHER/ARTIST:
Mela Ram Photographer, Peshawar

ATTOCK FORT.

TITLE:
Attock Fort

PRINTER/PUBLISHER:
Printed in Saxony

PHOTOGRAPHER/ARTIST:
Mela Ram Photographer, Peshawar

Attock Bridge with running train.

TITLE:
Attock Bridge with Running Train
PRINTER/PUBLISHER:
Printed in Saxony

Rawal Pindi Bazaar.

TITLE:
Rawal Pindi Bazaar
PRINTER/PUBLISHER:
Bremner Photo, Lahore and Quetta
POSTAL USAGE:
*Lahore (Pakistan) to Basel
(Switzerland), September 1925*

British Cavalry Barracks — Rawalpindi

TITLE:
*British Cavalry Barracks -
Rawalpindi*

PRINTER/PUBLISHER:
*Moorli Dhur & Sons, Ambala;
printed in Germany*

Best wishes for a Happy New Year.
1907.

R. S. MAYA SHAH & BROS

"CENTRE OF SUDDER BAZAR, RAWALPINDI.

TITLE:
Centre of Sudder Bazar, Rawalpindi

POSTAL USAGE:
To Lucknow (India), January 1907

NWFP, Punjab & Delhi

The Mall, Rawalpindi

THE MALL RAWALPINDI

TITLE:
The Mall, Rawalpindi
PRINTER/PUBLISHER:
Printed in Saxony

SHISH MAHAL FORT, LAHORE.

No. 24.   Shunker, Dass & Co., Lahore.

TITLE:
Shish Mahal Fort, Lahore
PRINTER/PUBLISHER:
*Shunker Dass & Co., Lahore;
printed in Saxony*

TITLE:
*Amritdhara Pharmacy,
Lahore (India)*

TITLE:
Lahore. Delhi Gate
PRINTER/PUBLISHER:
Raphael Tuck & Sons, London

CHIEFS COLLEGE, LAHORE.

No. 11.

TITLE:
Chiefs College, Lahore

PRINTER/PUBLISHER:
Shunker Dass & Co., Lahore

POSTAL USAGE:
Lucknow (India) to Paris (France), March 1911

Wazir Khan's Mosque, Lahore City.

TITLE:
Wazir Khan's Mosque, Lahore City

PRINTER/PUBLISHER:
Bremner Photo, Lahore and Quetta

UNDIVIDED BACK

Ranjit Singh's Tomb, Lahore Fort.

TITLE:
Ranjit Singh's Tomb, Lahore Fort
PRINTER/PUBLISHER:
Bremner Photo, Lahore and Quetta
UNDIVIDED BACK

JAHANGIR'S TOMB, SHADARA, LAHORE.

No. 8.   Shunker, Dass & Co., Lahore.

TITLE:
Jahangir's Tomb, Shadara, Lahore
PRINTER/PUBLISHER:
*Shunker Dass & Co., Lahore;
printed in Saxony*

TITLE:
Edga Musq, Mooltan
PRINTER/PUBLISHER:
Printed in England

TITLE:
Birdseye View - Amritsar
PRINTER/PUBLISHER:
*D.A. Ahuja, Rangoon;
printed in Germany*

Amritsar ; Golden Temple Gate and City

VINO DI CHINA FERRUGINOSO SERRAVALLO

J. SERRAVALLO
TRIESTE

TITLE:
Baba Atal, Amritsar

PRINTER/PUBLISHER:
Lal Singh & Co., Amritsar

TITLE:
Akal Bungha, Amritsar

PRINTER/PUBLISHER:
Lal Singh & Co., Amritsar

Kings Hotel Ambala

TITLE:
Kings Hotel Ambala

PRINTER/PUBLISHER:
Moorli Dhur & Sons, Ambala

Side View of B. Infantry Bazar Ambala

TITLE:
*Side View of B. Infantry
Bazar Ambala*

PRINTER/PUBLISHER:
*Moorli Dhur & Sons, Ambala;
printed in Germany*

The Saraghari Memorial, Ferozepore.

TITLE:
The Saraghari Memorial, Ferozepore

PRINTER/PUBLISHER:
Bremner Photo, Lahore and Quetta

The Memorial Gardens, Ferozepore.

TITLE:
The Memorial Gardens, Ferozepore

PRINTER/PUBLISHER:
Bremner Photo, Lahore and Quetta

NWFP, Punjab & Delhi

79

TITLE:
Brautzug (Einzug des Bräutigams)
bei der Hochzeit einer prinzessin
am hofe zu Patiala (Departure of
the bridegroom at the wedding of the
princess of Patiala)

PRINTER/PUBLISHER:
Wochenpost 1953, Austria;
printed in Austria

POSTAL USAGE:
Bombay (India) to
Vienna (Austria)

THEIR MAJESTIES THE KING AND QUEEN AND THE
KING AND QUEEN OF ROUMANIA IN PATIALA STATE COURT.

TITLE:
Their Majesties the King and Queen
and the King and Queen of Roumania
in Patiala State Court

PRINTER/PUBLISHER:
Raphael Tuck & Sons, London

PATIALA STATE COURT

TITLE:
Patiala State Court

PRINTER/PUBLISHER:
Raphael Tuck & Sons, London

(THE UNVEILING)
C.A WILES BRIGHTON

DEDICATION OF THE INDIAN MEMORIAL GATEWAY BY MAHARAJA OF PATIALA OCT-26-1921-

TITLE:
The Unveiling - Dedication of the Indian Memorial gateway by Maharaja of Patiala, Oct 26 1921

PRINTER/PUBLISHER:
Printed in England

PHOTOGRAPHER/ARTIST:
C.A Wiles, Brighton

H. E. the Raja's Palace Chumba near Dalhousie

TITLE:
H.E. the Raja's Palace Chumba near Dalhousie

PRINTER/PUBLISHER:
B.K. Abdul & Co., Ranikhet; printed in Saxony

General View Chamba Estate near Dalhousie

TITLE:
General View Chamba Estate near Dalhousie

PRINTER/PUBLISHER:
Printed in Saxony

General View of Kajiar.

TITLE:
General View of Kajiar
UNDIVIDED BACK

SUDDER BAZAAR OF DHARAMSALA AFTER EARTHQUAKE OF 4th APRIL, 1905

TITLE:
Sudder Bazar of Dharamsala after Earthquake of 4th April, 1905
UNDIVIDED BACK

Mc. Leod Gunge, Dharmsala.   J.&H. King, Simla.

TITLE:
McLeod Gunge, Dharmsala

PRINTER/PUBLISHER:
J&H. King, Simla

UNDIVIDED BACK

STONE MASONRY REVETEMENT COST OVER 1½ LAKHS.

TITLE:
*Stone Masonry Revetement
Cost over 1.5 Lakhs*

PRINTER/PUBLISHER:
*Moorli Dhur & Sons, Ambala;
printed in Germany*

TITLE:
The Highest Viaduct on the Kalka Simla Railway

POSTAL USAGE:
Simla (India) to Lincolnshire (UK), April 1909

7155. The Highest Viaduct on the Kalka Simla Railway

BEGINNING OF THE LINE. THE "S" KALKA IN THE DISTANCE.

TITLE:
Beginning of the Line: The 'S' Kalka in the Distance

PRINTER/PUBLISHER:
Moorli Dhur & Sons, Ambala; printed in England

Dagshai View.

TITLE:
Dagshai View

PRINTER/PUBLISHER:
*Moorli Dhur & Sons, Ambala;
printed in Germany*

PRINCIPAL STATION BAROGH, HALT FOR REFRESHMENTS

TITLE:
*Principal Station Barogh
Halt for Refreshments*

PRINTER/PUBLISHER:
Moorli Dhur & Sons, Ambala

POSTAL USAGE:
*Somerset (UK) to Devon (UK),
December 1924*

General View of Simla with Railway

TITLE:
General View of Simla with Railway

PRINTER/PUBLISHER:
*Moorli Dhur & Sons, Ambala;
printed in Germany*

CHRIST CHURCH, SIMLA.

Thacker, Spink & Co., Simla. India.

TITLE:
Christ Church, Simla

PRINTER/PUBLISHER:
Thacker, Spink & Co., Simla

UNDIVIDED BACK

Fire in Gunj — Simla

TITLE:
Fire in Gunj - Simla

PRINTER/PUBLISHER:
*Moorli Dhur & Sons, Ambala;
printed in Germany*

Secretariat Buildings.   Govt of India.   Simla.

With Hearty Greetings.   B. Dukoff Gordon

TITLE:
*Secretariat Buildings.
Govt of India. Simla*

UNDIVIDED BACK

POSTAL USAGE:
*Allahabad (India) to
Cleveland (USA), April 1906*

MONKEYS ON JAKKO. SIMLA.   Photo by W. Kennedy.

TITLE:
Monkeys on Jakko, Simla

PHOTOGRAPHER/ARTIST:
W. Kennedy

UNDIVIDED BACK

257.   Picturesque View of Simla, from "Bonnie Moon".

TITLE:
Picturesque View of Simla from "Bonnie Moon"

PRINTER/PUBLISHER:
The Arch. Photo - Works of India; printed in Brussels

NWFP, Punjab & Delhi

312. Grand Hôtel, Simla.

298. The Viceregal Lodge, Simla.

Tonga Terminus & Winterfield — Simla

TITLE:
Tonga Terminus &
Winterfield - Simla

PRINTER/PUBLISHER:
Moorli Dhur & Sons,
Ambala; printed in Germany

Barracks and Square, Kasauli from East

TITLE:
Barracks and Square.
Kasauli from East

PRINTER/PUBLISHER:
Moorli Dhur & Sons, Ambala;
printed in Germany

General View - Kasauli

TITLE:
General View - Kasauli

PRINTER/PUBLISHER:
*Moorli Dhur & Sons, Ambala;
printed in Germany*

60ᵗʰ Rifles. From Dagsbai To Ambala. Incidents Of The March.

Chandigarh Camp. General View - Oct. 1911

TITLE:
*Chandigarh Camp. General View.
Oct. 1911*

TITLE:
In Camp at Chandigarh, India,
22nd October 1911

TITLE:
Camel on the March.
Chandigarh 1911

BRIDGE OVER THE SUTLEJ AT WANGTU.

TITLE:
Bridge over the Sutlej at Wangtu

PRINTER/PUBLISHER:
Printed in Germany

UNDIVIDED BACK

POSTAL USAGE:

*To Rayapuram (India),
February 1905*

TITLE:
The Kutub, Delhi

PRINTER/PUBLISHER:
Clifton & Co., Bombay

UNDIVIDED BACK

On the postcard image, vertical text on left: Thacker, Spink & Co., Calcutta

THE KUTUB MINAR, DELHI.

Handwritten message:

Calcutta
19. 2. 03
My Dear
Bene
It is
too bad
only to
acknowledge
your kind
letter of
30 Jan
with a card
but I have
had a very
busy day and no time is now left
for a long and interesting letter,
au revoir marlyn.

TITLE:
The Kutub Minar, Delhi

PRINTER/PUBLISHER:
Thacker, Spink & Co., Calcutta

UNDIVIDED BACK

POSTAL USAGE:
*Calcutta (India) to London (UK),
February 1903*

Shamsuddeen
Altamash's
Tomb, Delhi

M. M. Gargh & Co., Agra

TITLE:
*Shamsuddeen Altamash's
Tomb, Delhi*

PRINTER/PUBLISHER:
M.M. Gargh & Co., Agra

Mayo Gate and Iron Pillar, Delhi.

52.

Indaraprasth (old Fort), Delhi

M. M. Gargh & Co., Agra

TITLE:
Indaraprasth (old Fort), Delhi
PRINTER/PUBLISHER:
M.M. Gargh & Co., Agra

A general view Tomb of emperor Tuglaq and Tuglaq Fort, Delhi.

TITLE:
*A General View Tomb of Emperor
Tuglaq and Tuglaq Fort, Delhi*
PRINTER/PUBLISHER:
*H.A. Mirza & Sons, Delhi;
printed in Germany*

TITLE:
Humajons Tomb, Delhi

PRINTER/PUBLISHER:
Raphael Tuck & Sons, London

TITLE:
Tomb of Khawja Kutbuddin Bakhtiar Kaki Chishti, Delhi

PRINTER/PUBLISHER:
H.A. Mirza & Sons, Delhi; printed in Germany

The Interior of Delhi Gate, Fort Delhi.

TITLE:
*The Interior of Delhi Gate,
Fort Delhi*

PRINTER/PUBLISHER:
*M.L. Sugan Chand, Delhi; printed
by Raphael Tuck & Sons, London*

Barracks in the Fort - Delhi

TITLE:
Barracks in the Fort - Delhi

PRINTER/PUBLISHER:
Dott. A. Baggio & Co., Torino, Italy

PHOTOGRAPHER/ARTIST:
Omed Singh & Pyarey Lall, Delhi

Throne of Dewan-i-Am, Fort Delhi.

TITLE:
Throne of Dewan-i-Am, Fort Delhi
PRINTER/PUBLISHER:
H.A. Mirza & Sons, Delhi;
printed in Germany

Interior Deewan Khas in Fort Delhi.

TITLE:
Interior Deewan Khas in Fort Delhi
PRINTER/PUBLISHER:
H.A. Mirza & Sons, Delhi;
printed in Germany

Interior Scale of Justice, Fort, Delhi.
Built by the Emperor Shahjahan between 1638 & 1648 A. D.

TITLE:
Interior Scale of Justice, Fort, Delhi.
Built by the Emperor Shahjahan
between 1638 & 1648 A. D.

PRINTER/PUBLISHER:
H.A. Mirza & Sons, Delhi;
printed in Germany

THE TOMB OF PRINCESS JAHANARA BEGAM. DELHI.

TITLE:
The Tomb of Princess Jahanara
Begam - Delhi

PRINTER/PUBLISHER:
The Arch. Photo - Works of India;
printed in Saxony

BIRD EYE VIEW OF THE CITY. DELHI.

TITLE:
Bird Eye View of the City. Delhi

PRINTER/PUBLISHER:
*H.A. Mirza & Sons, Delhi;
printed in Germany*

Birds eye view — the city with Juma Masjid, Delhi.

TITLE:
*Birds Eye View - the City with Juma
Masjid, Delhi*

PRINTER/PUBLISHER:
*H.A. Mirza & Sons, Delhi;
printed in Germany*

TITLE:
Jumnea Musjid - Delhi

PRINTER/PUBLISHER:
D.A. Ahuja, Rangoon;
printed in Germany

TITLE:
The Jumma Musjid - Delhi.
Friday Prayer Meeting

PRINTER/PUBLISHER:
Thacker, Spink & Co., Calcutta

UNDIVIDED BACK

POSTAL USAGE:
Calcutta (India) to London (UK),
December 1902

Clock Tower chandni Chowk, Delhi.
Built by Delhi Municipality at a Cost of R. 28000, after the Mutiny 1857 A. D.

TITLE:
*Clock Tower Chandni Chowk,
Delhi. Built by Delhi Municipality
at a cost of R 28000 after the
Mutiny 1857 A. D.*

PRINTER/PUBLISHER:
*H.A. Mirza & Sons, Delhi;
printed in Germany*

No. 71. CHANDNI CHAWK STREET, DELHI (INDIA).

TITLE:
*Chandni Chawk Street,
Delhi (India)*

PRINTER/PUBLISHER:
*H.A. Mirza & Sons, Delhi;
printed in Germany*

POSTAL USAGE:
*Within Bombay (India),
November 1927*

TITLE:
Bazar, Chandni Chowk, Delhi

PRINTER/PUBLISHER:
Moorli Dhur & Sons, Ambala; printed in Germany

TITLE:
Railway Station, Delhi

PRINTER/PUBLISHER:
Hernam Dass & Sons, Ambala; printed in Germany

JANTER MANTER OR OBSERVATORY, DELHI.

TITLE:
Janter Manter or Observatory, Delhi

PRINTER/PUBLISHER:
*H.A. Mirza & Sons, Delhi;
printed in Germany*

TITLE:
Connaught Circus

Cecil Hotel, Delhi.

TITLE:
Cecil Hotel, Delhi

PRINTER/PUBLISHER:
Printed in Saxony

PHOTOGRAPHER/ARTIST
Lal Chand & Sons, Delhi

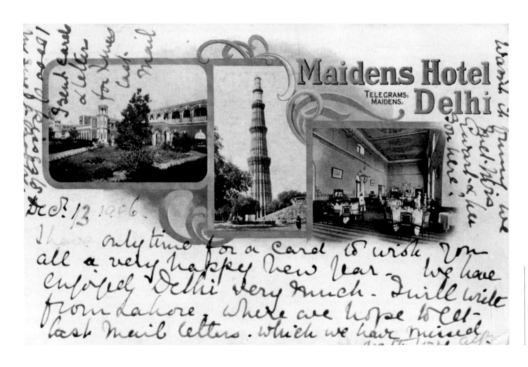

TITLE:
Maidens Hotel, Delhi

UNDIVIDED BACK

POSTAL USAGE:
*Delhi (India) to London (UK),
December 1906*

Visit **IMRE SCHWAIGER'S ART MUSEUM,**
(Opposite MAIDEN'S HOTEL)
8, ALIPORE ROAD, DELHI.

TITLE:
Visit Imre Schwaiger's Art Museum,
(Opposite Maiden's Hotel)
8, Alipore Road, Delhi

The Delhi Church

TITLE:
The Delhi Church

PRINTER/PUBLISHER:
Dott. A. Baggio & Co., Torino, Italy

PHOTOGRAPHER/ARTIST
Omed Singh & Pyarey Lall, Delhi

TITLE:
Memorial old Telegraph office, Delhi

PRINTER/PUBLISHER:
H.A. Mirza & Sons, Delhi;
printed in Germany

TITLE:
Secretariat Building Capital,
Delhi, (India)

PRINTER/PUBLISHER:
Printed in England

No. 56. THE SECRETARIATS OF THE GOVERNMENT OF INDIA. DELHI

TITLE:
The Secretariats of the Government of India, Delhi

PRINTER/PUBLISHER:
H.A. Mirza & Sons, Delhi; printed in Saxony

Both Secretariats & Viceroy House, New Delhi

TITLE:
Both Secretariats & Viceroy House, New Delhi

PRINTER/PUBLISHER:
Printed in Saxony

PHOTOGRAPHER/ARTIST:
Lal Chand & Sons, Delhi

THE DELHI DÙRBAR. — THE IMPERIAL CADET CORPS.

TITLE:
The Delhi Durbar.
The Imperial Cadet Corps

PHOTOGRAPHER/ARTIST:
Jadu Kissen, Delhi

UNDIVIDED BACK

POSTAL USAGE:
India to Cleveland (USA),
June 1906

Coronation Durbar 1911 - Delhi.
Coronation Scene

TITLE:
Coronation Durbar 1911 - Delhi.
Coronation Scene

PRINTER/PUBLISHER:
H.A. Mirza & Sons, Delhi;
printed in Germany

The Delhi Coronation Durbar

TITLE:
The Delhi Coronation Durbar

1885. Photo Wiele & Klein.

Durbar Delhi. The Viceroy in front. T. R. H. the Duke and Duchess of Connaught starting from Railway Station to open the Procession.

TITLE:
Durbar Delhi. The Viceroy in front. T.R.H. the Duke and Duchess of Connaught starting from Railway Station to open procession

PRINTER/PUBLISHER:
Printed in Germany

PHOTOGRAPHER/ARTIST:
Wiele and Klein

UNDIVIDED BACK

NWFP, Punjab & Delhi

KASHMIR

&

UNITED PROVINCES

LA POSTA NEL CACHEMIRE

The captivating beauty of the Kashmir Valley surrounded by the snowy outer ranges of the Himalayas and the Karakoram, with its unique flora and fauna, the sports facilities and the excellent weather in summer, made it a favourite tourist spot for the Europeans residing in India. Trips were organised beyond Srinagar by road to the upper plateaus of Gulmarg or to Leh through Sonamarg and the Zojila Pass. Boats took travellers up the river Jhelum to Islamabad, the second largest city of Kashmir at that time, and from there road trips were made to Pahalgam at the end of the Liddar Valley and to the Amarnath caves.

Till the early 1900s, Srinagar was only connected by road from Rawalpindi, Gujrat and Abbottabad. Efforts were on during the Golden Era of picture postcards to construct a railway line from Rawalpindi to Srinagar through Murree and Baramulla running on electric power generated from the Jhelum Falls. Railway lines were also proposed to be extended to Jammu.

Picture postcards of Kashmir during the Golden Era captured the natural scenery of the state, with houseboats drifting on the picturesque Dal Lake, the old wooden bridges, the historic sights of Srinagar such as the Sher Garhi palace of the erstwhile maharajas, Akbar's fort on Hari Parbat Hill, the numerous gardens built by the Mughals, the wooden Jama Masjid mosque, Takht-i-Suleiman and other scattered archaeological ruins that bore traces of Greek influence.

Rawal Pindi to Srinagar (Kashmere):

Rawal Pindi ...	Flashman's Hotel	Good	—
Murree ...	Several hotels	—	—
Dewal ...	Dâk Bungalow	Fair	No supplies
Kohala Ferry	,,	,,	Supplies doubtful
Dulai	,,	Small	,,
Dumel, or Mosaferabad	,,	Large and new	Supplies
Garhi	,,	Large and new	,,
Hatti	,,	—	Supplies doubtful
Chagoti ...	,,	Very bad	No supplies
Uri	,,	Large and new	Supplies
Rampore ...	,,	Old and dirty	Supplies doubtful
Baramulla ...	,,	Large and new	Supplies
Srinagar ...	,,	New and good	,,

N.B.—Bread and soda-water are difficult to obtain in many of these dâk bungalows.

Hotels and dak bungalows en route Rawalpindi to Srinagar listed in the book Motoring in India: A Guide for the Tourist and Resident, *by Charles Watney and Mrs Herbert Lloyd, published by Car Illustrated Ltd, London, 1909*

The Kashmir Valley was drained by the Jhelum and Kishenganga Rivers, with the range of low hills in southern Kashmir leading to the vast expanse of the Ganga and Yamuna river plains in the United Provinces of Agra and Oudh, created by the British in 1902. Populated by every 30th person in the world today, between 1856 and 1902, this region existed as two separate provinces: North-Western Provinces and Oudh (from Ayodhya to Ayudh to Awadh to Oudh). Allahabad was made the first capital in 1902, with the capital shifting back to Lucknow in 1920. The shortened name of United Provinces came into use from 1935 and was changed to Uttar Pradesh (UP) in 1950. The nine administrative divisions of the

United Provinces under the British were: Meerut, Agra, Allahabad, Lucknow, Faizabad, Rohilkhand, Benares, Gorakhpur and Kumaon. UP still remains united as a state within India even though the mountains of Kumaon and Garhwal (which bordered Kashmir) have been carved out as the separate Uttarakhand state.

The EIC had created several cantonments (army bases) on the outskirts of towns, both in the hills and plains, prominent among them being Meerut, Bareilly, Agra, Allahabad, Roorkee, Ranikhet and Chakrata, to name a few. Most of them had a clearly marked "Civil Lines" area for the European residents, distinct from its "Cantt" and "Native" residential areas. The growth of cantonments, captured in picture postcards, was strategically important for the war plans to win territory from various Indian kings. Immediately after 1857, the British India government realised the need to link these 50 odd cantonments across the country through land and rail routes, and much of this was actually achieved by 1890. In the United Provinces, the Indian Midland Railway line connected Delhi to Agra through Muttra. Meerut was connected through the North-Western Railway line. Kanpur was well connected, being the junction of four railway lines: East Indian Railway, Cawnpore-Achnera Railway line, the Indian Midland Railway line and the North-Western Bengal Railway.

Many of the postcards of Kanpur and Lucknow carry the memory of the Indian War of Independence of 1857 (referred to as the "Mutiny" by the Europeans), featuring memorials built by the British to commemorate the soldiers who fought and died in the War. A postcard in this series "Jessie's dream at Lucknow" shows English women and children hiding in the basement of the British Residency at Lucknow during the siege of 1857, with Indian soldiers that were led by Begum Hazrat Mahal shown as trying to enter from the back. Jessie Brown was believed to be the wife of a British soldier stationed at Lucknow. Right through the five months of siege, she kept the morale high of all the British soldiers and their families trapped within the Residency. On the last evening before the siege was broken by the British, while suffering from high fever, Jessie was believed to have dreamt of the arrival of their rescuers along with the sound of bagpipes. This was just when

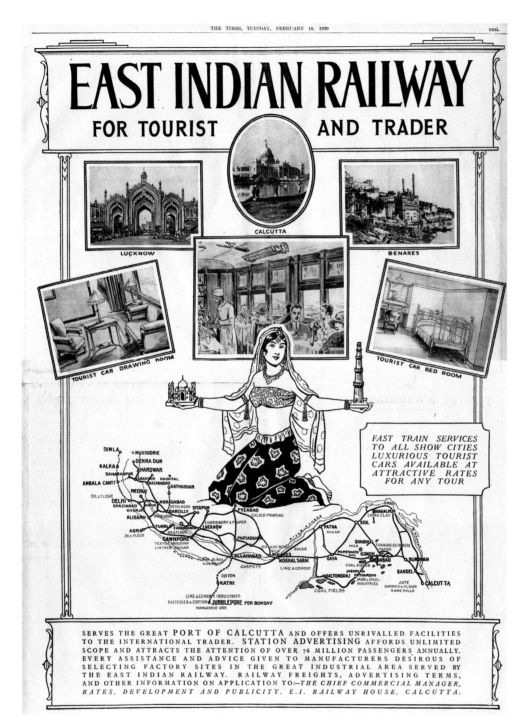

East India Railway
advertisement published
in the The Times, 18
February 1930

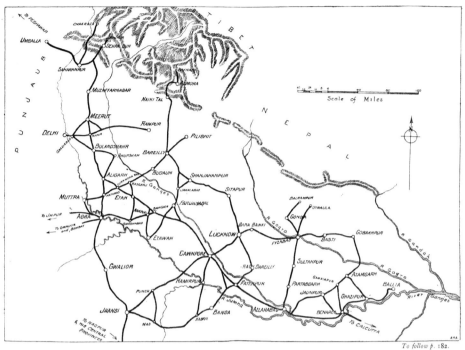

To follow p. 182.

Road map of the United Provinces published in the book Motoring in India: A Guide for the Tourist and Resident

the British at the Residency were contemplating surrender. They were egged on not to give up and the very next day itself the Highland Regiment, led by Major General Henry Havelock, did storm into the Residency, finally taking it back from the Indians. This much-loved story that helped the British secure Lucknow once again was recreated as poetry, prose, drama, sheet music, on postcards and even painted on porcelain. Other postcards of Lucknow feature this city of palaces and gardens centred around the "Chowk" that came up on the southern bank of the river Gomti as the capital of the nawabs of Awadh shifted here from Faizabad in 1775. Several of the baroque and early Gothic buildings for the nawabs and the EIC were designed by Major General Claude Martin (1735–1800), best known as the founder of the La Martiniere School, featured in this series.

Lucknow and Bareilly were connected by the Oudh and Rohilkand Railway line running between Saharanpur and Benares. Allahabad was connected to Calcutta

Kashmir & United Provinces

121

through the East Indian Railway. The Kumaon region was the retreat in the summer months and its urban development was popularised through postcards. Bareilly Junction was the base to start the journey to the Kumaon region with the Rohilkhand-Kumaon Railway line terminating at Kathgodam. Like today, travellers proceeded uphill by road to Nainital via Rambagh and Douglas Dale. Dehradun was reached from Haridwar and travellers proceeded to Mussoorie via Rajpur and Jarapani. The hill cantonment of Chakrata was on the road connecting Mussoorie to the summer capital Simla. These picturesque hill journeys, undertaken on ponies or *tonga*s, feature abundantly in picture postcards.

The newly built public and administrative buildings of the provinces were well captured in postcards. One of the first churches of northern India, St. John's Church, was built by the British in Meerut as early as 1821. Featured in this section are the postcards of the Saracenic-styled Muir Central College at Allahabad, which was the chief educational establishment of the North-Western Provinces, and the Queens College in Benares, which housed important Buddhist and Hindu remains from Sarnath. Images of the exotic Orient sent to friends and relatives across the world through picture postcards from this province conveyed the grandeur of the Awadh kingdom, the splendour of the Mughal carvings, the *jali* and pietra dura marble inlay work. Postcards featured the views of the sacred cities that lay on the banks of the rivers Yamuna and Ganga: Mathura, Brindaban (Vrindavan), Allahabad and, most of all, Benares. The postcards feature the temples, ghats, the "fakirs", havelis and bazaars. The picturesque was sketched by hand or captured through photographs while sailing along the ghats at dawn or dusk, observing the Hindu prayers or cremation rites being conducted by the priests on the ghat steps against the backdrop of the city. Clark's Hotel was considered the best in Benares at that time to stay in or to enjoy a tour of the city with the hotel's tour guides.

The Spinning Wheel.

TITLE:
The Spinning Wheel
UNDIVIDED BACK

Nishat Bagh, Kashmir

TITLE:
Nishat Bagh, Kashmir

Srinuggur, From Safoola Baba's House

TITLE:
Srinuggur, from Safoola Baba's House

PRINTER/PUBLISHER:
Printed in Luxembourg

PHOTOGRAPHER/ARTIST:
The Phototype Co., Bombay

POSTAL USAGE:
From Bombay (India)

Srinagar, looking towards the Palace.

TITLE:
Srinagar, looking towards the Palace

PRINTER/PUBLISHER:
Bremner Photo, Lahore and Quetta

UNDIVIDED BACK

The Dhal Lake, Kashmir.

TITLE:
The Dhal Lake, Kashmir

PRINTER/PUBLISHER:
Bremner Photo, Lahore and Quetta

UNDIVIDED BACK

View from Takht towards River Jhelum, Srinagar, Kashmir

TITLE:
View from Takht towards River Jhelum, Srinagar, Kashmir

General View of the city, Fort and the Mosque, Kashmere.

TITLE:
General View of the City, Fort and the Mosque, Kashmere

PRINTER/PUBLISHER:
H.A. Mirza & Sons, Delhi; printed in Germany

No. 2. **Harising High Street, Srinagar, Kashmir**   Dutta, Kashmir

TITLE:
Harising High Street, Srinagar, Kashmir

PRINTER/PUBLISHER:
Dutta, Kashmir

No. 4.   Ist Bridge, Amirakadal, Srinagar, Kashmir   Dutta, Kashmir

TITLE:
1st Bridge, Amirakadal,
Srinagar, Kashmir

PRINTER/PUBLISHER:
Dutta, Kashmir

SRINAGAR. A SHOOTING PARTY IN CAMP.   SR 956.

TITLE:
Srinagar. A Shooting
Party in Camp

PRINTER/PUBLISHER:
D. Macropolo & Co., Calcutta;
printed in Germany

No. 3. **Shergarhi Palaces, Srinagar, Kashmir**   Dutta Kashmir

TITLE:
*Shergarhi Palaces,
Srinagar, Kashmir*

PRINTER/PUBLISHER:
Dutta, Kashmir

GULMARG. GENERAL VIEW.   GL 959.

TITLE:
Gulmarg. General View

PRINTER/PUBLISHER:
*D. Macropolo & Co., Calcutta;
printed in Germany*

Islamabad, Kashmir.

TITLE:
Islamabad, Kashmir
PRINTER/PUBLISHER:
Bremner Photo, Lahore and Quetta
UNDIVIDED BACK

Lidar Valley and River, Kashmir.

TITLE:
Lidar Valley and River, Kashmir
PRINTER/PUBLISHER:
Bremner Photo, Lahore and Quetta
UNDIVIDED BACK

Amarnath Pilgrims' Camp Pahlgam, Kashmir

TITLE:
Amarnath Pilgrims' Camp Pahlgam, Kashmir

The Bazaar, Leh

TITLE:
The Bazaar, Leh
PRINTER/PUBLISHER:
R.E. Shooter, Sialkote and Kashmir
UNDIVIDED BACK

Mahatta & Co.   No. B 49   View looking over Leh (Kashmir)

TITLE:
View Looking over Leh (Kashmir)

PRINTER/PUBLISHER:
Mahatta & Co.; printed in Saxony

TITLE:
Govind Dev Ji Temple, Brindaban

TITLE:
Muttra - Street Scene

PRINTER/PUBLISHER:
*The Phototype Co., Bombay;
printed in Luxembourg*

TITLE:
The Bathing Ghat, Muttra

PRINTER/PUBLISHER:
The Great Indian Peninsula
Railway, Bombay

TITLE:
Agra City

PRINTER/PUBLISHER:
Clifton & Co., Bombay

UNDIVIDED BACK

General view of Pearl Mosque and Deewan-Am in Fort Agra.

TITLE:
Gateway of Etmaduddaula

PRINTER/PUBLISHER:
Printed in Saxony

PHOTOGRAPHER/ARTIST:
Lal Chand & Sons, Delhi

MAUSOLEUM OF PRINCE ITMAD-OOD-DOWLAH - AGRA.

Calcutta 25-12-02 my Dear Ida Gratefl thank for your Card and good wishes for Xmas. I hope you all had a good time Your affect Uncle — Wallie

TITLE:
Mausoleum of Prince Itmad-ood-dowlah - Agra

PRINTER/PUBLISHER:
Thacker, Spink & Co., Calcutta

UNDIVIDED BACK

POSTAL USAGE:
Calcutta (India) to London (UK), December 1902

Muhammedans at Prayer at the Jumma Masjid, Agra.

TITLE:
Muhammedans at Prayer at the Jumma Masjid, Agra

PRINTER/PUBLISHER:
The International P.P.C Club, Allahabad

POSTAL USAGE:
Allahabad (India) to Cleveland (USA), May 1908

EXTREME LEFT:

TITLE:
Agra Fort - Rosewater Bath

PHOTOGRAPHER/ARTIST:
K. Lall & Co., Agra

UNDIVIDED BACK

LEFT:

TITLE:
Agra

PRINTER/PUBLISHER:
Priya Lall & Sons, Agra Cantt

UNDIVIDED BACK

TITLE:
Secundra, Agra

PRINTER/PUBLISHER:
Printed in Germany

POSTAL USAGE:
*To Liberec (Czech Republic) ,
December 1913*

TITLE:
*Buland Gate
(Fatehpur Sekree), Agra*

PRINTER/PUBLISHER:
*H.A. Mirza & Sons, Delhi;
printed in Germany*

Cemetery, Meerutt (India).

TITLE:
Cemetery, Meerutt (India)

PRINTER/PUBLISHER:
*H.A. Mirza & Sons, Delhi;
printed in Germany*

Weeler Club, Meerutt (India).

TITLE:
Weeler Club, Meerutt (India)

PRINTER/PUBLISHER:
*H.A. Mirza & Sons, Delhi;
printed in Germany*

Picturesque India

TITLE:
Meerut - Roman Catholic Church
PRINTER/PUBLISHER:
Nestor Gianaclis Ltd, Calcutta

TITLE:
Town Hall. Meerut
POSTAL USAGE:
c. 1920s

TITLE:
Cawnpore. Memorial Church

PRINTER/PUBLISHER:
*D. Macropolo & Co., Calcutta;
printed in Germany*

TITLE:
Massacre Ghat. Cawnpore

No. 127   Statue Memorial Well, Cawnpore   M. M. G. A.

TITLE:
Statue Memorial Well, Cawnpore

PRINTER/PUBLISHER:
Printed in Germany

TITLE:
Jessie's Dream at Lucknow

PRINTER/PUBLISHER:
Printed in Bavaria

UNDIVIDED BACK

POSTAL USAGE:
Surat (India) to Teplice (Czech Republic), June 1920

Calcutta 1—1—03

Thacker, Spink & Co., Calcutta.

THE BAILEY GUARD GATE — LUCKNOW.

My Dear Winnie — Here is the other one !!! Yours truly

TITLE:
The Bailey Guard Gate - Lucknow

PRINTER/PUBLISHER:
Thacker, Spink & Co., Calcutta

UNDIVIDED BACK

POSTAL USAGE:
*Calcutta (India) to London (UK),
January 1903*

THE GREAT EMMEMBARA, LUCKNOW.

TITLE:
The Great Emmembara, Lucknow

PRINTER/PUBLISHER:
Printed in Germany

PHOTOGRAPHER/ARTIST
*S.H. Dagg, Allahabad
and Mussoorie*

UNDIVIDED BACK

Lucknow, Rumi Darwaza

TITLE:
Lucknow, Rumi Darwaza

PRINTER/PUBLISHER:
The Phototype Co., Bombay; printed in Luxembourg

View of Turkish Gate & Entrance Gate of Imambara, Lucknow

TITLE:
View of Turkish Gate & Entrance Gate of Imambara, lucknow

PRINTER/PUBLISHER:
Printed in Saxony

La Martiniere, Lucknow

HOSSEINABAD GARDEN & TANK — LUCKNOW.

Thacker, Spink & Co., Calcutta.

TITLE:
*Hosseinabad Garden &
Tank - Lucknow*

PRINTER/PUBLISHER:
Thacker, Spink & Co., Calcutta

UNDIVIDED BACK

POSTAL USAGE:
*Calcutta (India) to Lucknow
(India), December 1902*

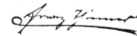

Souvenir of East Indies 75

TITLE:
Souvenir of East Indies - Allahabad
PRINTER/PUBLISHER:
Weltreise Verlag Compagnie Comet, Fr. Th & Co., Dresden
UNDIVIDED BACK

Bathing scene at the Confluence of the Jumna & Ganges.

JULIAN RUST, Art Photographer, Allahabad, Mussoorie, Landour & Meerut.

TITLE:
Bathing Scene at the Confluence of the Jumna & Ganges
PHOTOGRAPHER/ARTIST:
Julian Rust, Allahabad, Mussoorie, Landour and Meerut
UNDIVIDED BACK

A bit of the City, Allahabad

THE MUIR CENTRAL COLLEGE. ALLAHABAD.   J. Shapoorjee & Co., Allahabad & Naini Tal. 1730

Kushro-Bagh.   Allahabad.

TITLE:
Kushro-Bagh. Allahabad

PRINTER/PUBLISHER:
Printed in Germany

PHOTOGRAPHER/ARTIST:
S.H. Dagg, Allahabad and Mussoorie

UNDIVIDED BACK

High School, Bareilly.

TITLE:
High School, Bareilly

PRINTER/PUBLISHER:
Hernam Dass & Sons, Ambala and Dagshai; printed abroad

Bird's-eye View of Naini Tal.

PARSI SAH, PHOTOGRAPHER, NAINI TAL.

TITLE:
Bird's-eye View of Naini Tal

PHOTOGRAPHER/ARTIST:
Parsi Sah, Naini Tal

UNDIVIDED BACK

SECRETARIAT OFFICE, NAINI TAL.

TITLE:
Secretariat Office, Naini Tal

PRINTER/PUBLISHER:
The Collectors' Publishing Co., London

UNDIVIDED BACK

POSTAL USAGE:
Mussoorie (India) to Cleveland (USA), c. June 1905

Naina Davi Temple, Naini Tal.   *Souvenirs*   PARSI SAH, PHOTOGRAPHER, NAINI TAL

TITLE:
Naina Davi Temple, Naini Tal

PHOTOGRAPHER/ARTIST:
Parsi Sah, Naini Tal

UNDIVIDED BACK

POSTAL USAGE:
Nainital (India) to Canton de Geneve (Switzerland), July 1906

The Club, Naini Tal

TITLE:
The Club, Naini Tal

UNDIVIDED BACK

POSTAL USAGE:
June 1906

The Lake and Cheena Peak, Naini Tal   No. 2

TITLE:
The Lake and Cheena Peak, Naini Tal

PRINTER/PUBLISHER:
Reynolds & Co., Naini Tal; printed in England

The Club, Dehra Doon.

TITLE:
The Club, Dehra Doon

PRINTER/PUBLISHER:
Julian Rust, Allahabad, Mussoorie, Landour and Meerut

Kashmir & United Provinces

"Catching wild Elephants Near Dehra Doon."

TITLE:
Catching Wild Elephants near Dehra Doon

PRINTER/PUBLISHER:
Julian Rust, Allahabad, Mussoorie, Landour and Meerut

Rajpur Tonga Terminus for Mussoorie.

TITLE:
Rajpur Tonga Terminus for Mussoorie

HALF WAY HOUSE, MUSSOORI.

TITLE:
Half Way House. Mussoori

PRINTER/PUBLISHER:
Moorli Dhur & Sons, Ambala

THE MALL. MUSSOORIE.

TITLE:
The Mall. Mussoorie

PRINTER/PUBLISHER:
Printed in Saxony

Kulri Bazaar, Mussoorie.

TITLE:
Kulri Bazaar, Mussoorie

PRINTER/PUBLISHER:
Clifton & Co.,
Bombay; printed in Belgium

Regt. in Camp on the Parade Ground, Chakrata

TITLE:
Regt. in Camp on the Parade
Ground, Chakrata

PRINTER/PUBLISHER:
Moorli Dhur & Sons, Ambala;
printed in Germany

PHOTOGRAPHER/ARTIST:
Thos. H. Bell

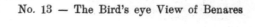

No. 13 — The Bird's eye View of Benares

No. 1 — The Temple on ganges, Benares

TITLE:
The Temple on Ganges, Benares
PRINTER/PUBLISHER:
Saeed Bros, Benares

No. 9 — Aurangzeb's Mosque at Burhma ghat, Benares

TITLE:
Aurangzeb's Mosque at Burhma Ghat, Benares
PRINTER/PUBLISHER:
Saeed Bros, Benares

Queens College, Benares.

TITLE:
Queens College, Benares
UNDIVIDED BACK

No. 15   The Well of Knowledge Benares

TITLE:
The Well of Knowledge, Benares
PRINTER/PUBLISHER:
Saeed Bros, Benares

THE LOUNGE CLARK'S HOTEL BENARES

TITLE:
The Lounge Clark's Hotel Benares
UNDIVIDED BACK

DASSAMEDH CHAT, BENARES.

TITLE:
Dassamedh Ghat, Benares
PRINTER/PUBLISHER:
*Raphael Tuck & Sons, London;
printed in England*

MESSAGERIES MARITIMES

BÉNARÈS
D'après l'aquarelle de M. Gilbert GALLAND

TITLE:
Messageries Maritimes - Benares

PRINTER/PUBLISHER:
Bernard Freres, Paris

PHOTOGRAPHER/ARTIST:
M. Gilbert Galland

No. 20 — Budhist ruines excavated at "Sarnath" — Benares

TITLE:
Budhist Ruines Excavated at "Sarnath" - Benares

PRINTER/PUBLISHER:
Saeed Bros, Benares

BALUCHISTAN

SINDH

RAJPUTANA

&

GUJARAT

Postmen of the British Empire:
Mail Carrier and Guard, Oudeypore, India.

FACING PAGE:

Postcard titled "Postmen of the British Empire: Mail Carrier and Guard, Oudeypore, India"

RIGHT:

An advertisement in The Times, *March 23, 1957, of the Air Services being offered by Tata Enterprises since 1932, for flying mail, passengers and freight between Karachi and Madras via Ahmedabad, Bombay and Hyderabad, and between Bombay and Trivandrum. These domestic flights offered connections to the international Imperial Airways flights arriving from and departing to Europe. This was the only airmail service of the British Empire that was not subsidised by the Government*

Baluchistan, Sindh, Rajputana and Gujarat were one continuous culture for more than a thousand years, with the years 1890 to 1947 being the final phase of this continuity. The sudden partitioning of the land in 1947 is evident from the popular land and rail routes that had prevailed during the British period and which were still listed in all the popular travel guides, including John Murray & Co. and Thomas Cook & Co., well into the 1950s. Eventually, they suggested airways as the solution.

The ethnography of the Baluchi- and Brahui (Dravidian language)-speaking people, the growing cantonments and the civilian urban development in Karachi and Quetta during the British time is captured well in the picture postcards of Baluchistan and Sindh. Karachi, the main city of Sindh, became a new and increasingly important landing port for international commercial trade and for the

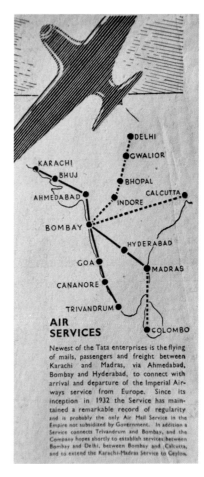

AIR SERVICES

Newest of the Tata enterprises is the flying of mails, passengers and freight between Karachi and Madras, via Ahmedabad, Bombay and Hyderabad, to connect with arrival and departure of the Imperial Airways service from Europe. Since its inception in 1932 the Service has maintained a remarkable record of regularity and is probably the only Air Mail Service in the Empire not subsidized by Government. In addition a Service connects Trivandrum and Bombay, and the Company hopes shortly to establish services between Bombay and Delhi, between Bombay and Calcutta, and to extend the Karachi-Madras Service to Ceylon.

European passenger steamers travelling through the Persian Gulf. Karachi was connected to Lahore and Mooltan by the Indus Valley Railway and the opening of these railway routes connected undivided Punjab, North-West India and Baluchistan. Postcards also capture the construction of the nearly mile-long Lloyd Barrage at Sukkur, across the Indus River, that had begun in 1923 for bringing the surrounding desert region into cultivation through enhanced irrigation.

The painters and photographers captured the "picturesque" in colourful Rajputana and Gujarat, as they witnessed the grandeur and generosity of the maharajas. Many of the early lithographic print and photographic postcards sent to friends and family in Europe featured their richly decorated palaces, the traditional rituals at temples, the colourful city streets lined with bazaars and town houses decorated with elaborate *chhatri* and latticed window patterns. The camels and caravans in the desert, the landscape scattered with natural and man-made lakes and tanks, and surrounding hills dotted with imposing forts watching over the towns spread out below them were the common subjects in early picture postcards of this region.

The Bombay, Baroda and Central Indian Railway (BB&CI) connected Delhi to Bombay in 34½ hours, passing through the princely states of the Rajputana Province and Gujarat. The Maharaja's Dak Bungalow at Bharatpur en route offered travellers free accommodation for the first 24 hours. Further on came Jaipur, the most prosperous city of the province, featured in a large number of postcards with its palaces and symmetrically laid out, wide and busy shop-lined streets full of exquisite handmade artefacts. Further on, Ajmer, the administrative headquarters of the British province of Ajmer-Merwara, is captured in postcards with its intricately carved facades of Altamash's Adhai-din-ka-Jhonpra, believed to have been converted from a Jain temple to a mosque in two and a half days, and the *Dilkhusha* gateway of the dargah built by Akbar and Shah Jahan.

The line to Jodhpur, the largest of the Rajputana states, ran from Marwar Junction and Bikaner. As a respite from the heat of the Central Indian Plains, Mount Abu,

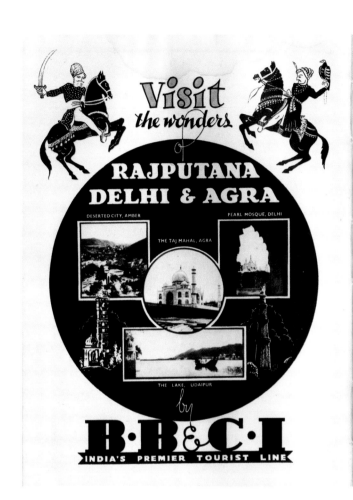

A spread from The Handbook of India, *2nd edition, issued by The Central Publicity Bureau, Railway Board, Delhi, c.1950, advertising travel to the Rajputana Province with the BB&CI Railway*

the headquarters of the Rajputana administration, became a popular excursion reached through the BB&CI Railway line by getting off at Abu Road Station and ascending the scenic road upto Mount Abu in about four hours. Udaipur was not connected to the railway network till the 1900s and travellers had to get off at Chittor Station to reach Udaipur by road.

The ruins of Rudra Mahalaya, the famous 10th-century Shiva temples of Gujarat, is featured in the picture postcard of Sidhpur. This was the only part of the Bombay Presidency where poppies were allowed to be grown and from which opium was manufactured at the State Stores of Sidhpur. From Sidhpur, the Delhi to Bombay line of the BB&CI continued to Ahmedabad, well captured in picture postcards with its beautiful temples, mosques, tombs and stepwells, all with richly carved exteriors, believed to combine elements of Islamic, Hindu and Jain architecture.

From Ahmedabad, the BB&CI Railway continued to Anand, Baroda and Surat before arriving at Bombay. At Baroda, the Indo-Saracenic-styled Laxmi Vilas Palace of the Gaekwars had just been built in the late 1800s and became a popular subject in several postcards of the Golden Era. By this time, Surat, where, along with Masulipatam, the first trading factories of the EIC were established and which stayed the most prominent port city of India during the 15th to the 18th centuries, had already been superseded by Bombay.

The BB&CI Railway line from Ahmedabad to the remote Kathiawar Peninsula was extended in the 1880s, thereby becoming an increasingly important connecting link with the newly opened Port Okha in the Gulf of Cutch (Kutch). Coming from Ahmedabad, the train crossed a bridge, with a footway for passengers fixed alongside and carrying the rails for both broad and narrow gauges. The narrow gauge continued north to Delhi and Agra, while the broad gauge turned West towards Kathiawar, passing through the prominent towns of Bhavnagar, Junagarh and Somnath, some part of the journey facilitated by the Bhavnagar-Gondal Railway. Bhavnagar Port became one of the principal centres for export of Kathiawar cotton. From the station of Songad, 24 km south by road were the Jain Temples of Palitana where hundreds of shrines were spread across the holy mountain of Shatrunjaya. Further on the Bhavnagar-Gondal Railway, a branch line from Jetalsar connected to Rajkot.

Cantonment Market, Quetta.

TITLE:
Cantonment Market, Quetta

PRINTER/PUBLISHER:
R.W. Rai & Sons, Quetta;
printed in Germany

BIRD'S EYE VIEW. KARACHI

TITLE:
Bird's Eye View. Karachi

PRINTER/PUBLISHER:
A. Hajee Dossul & Sons

POSTAL USAGE:
Karachi (Pakistan) to
Vienna (Austria), December 1911

Baluchistan, Sindh, Rajputana & Gujarat

General's Bungalow and Barracks, Karachi.

TITLE:
General's Bungalow and Barracks, Karachi

PHOTOGRAPHER/ARTIST:
Byramjee Eduljee, Karachi

POSTAL USAGE:
Karachi (Pakistan) to Bremen (Germany), April 1908

Bremner Lahore and Quetta

On the Indus, looking towards Sukkur Bridge.

TITLE:
On the Indus, looking towards Sukkur Bridge

PRINTER/PUBLISHER:
Bremner Photo, Lahore and Quetta

UNDIVIDED BACK

GENERAL VIEW, BHURT PORE.

TITLE:
General View, Bhurt Pore

PRINTER/PUBLISHER:
Printed in Germany

UNDIVIDED BACK

Gobindram Oodeyram, Artists, Jaipur.

Elephant Fight, Jaipur

TITLE:
Elephant Fight, Jaipur

PRINTER/PUBLISHER:
Printed in Germany

PHOTOGRAPHER/ARTIST:
*Gobindram Oodeyram
Artists, Jaipur*

Gobindram Oodeyram, Jaipur.   Main street.   Jaipur.

TITLE:
Main Street. Jaipur

PHOTOGRAPHER/ARTIST:
Gobindram Oodeyram Artists, Jaipur

C. & O. JAIPUR.   A PARTY OF SOLDIERS CLAD IN COATS OF MAIL.

TITLE:
A Party of Soldiers Clad in Coats of Mail

PHOTOGRAPHER/ARTIST:
Gobindram Oodeyram Artists, Jaipur

UNDIVIDED BACK

THE GIRLS COLLEGE IN JEYPORE.

Verlanget und trinket nur Pekarek's China Thee!

TITLE:
The Girls College in Jeypore

PHOTOGRAPHER/ARTIST:
Joseph Hoffmann

UNDIVIDED BACK

POSTAL USAGE:
Vienna (Austria) to the Czech Republic, December 1904

View of Ajmere.

TITLE:
View of Ajmere

PRINTER/PUBLISHER:
Printed in Saxony

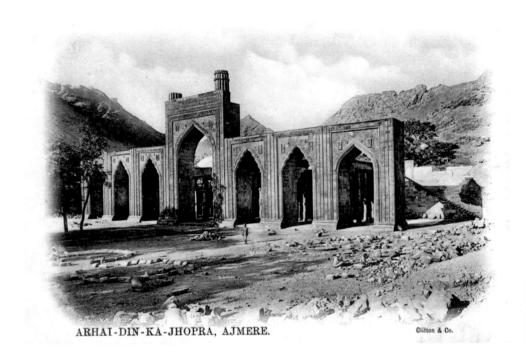

ARHAI-DIN-KA-JHOPRA, AJMERE.

Clifton & Co.

TITLE:
Arhai-din-ka-Jhopra, Ajmere
PRINTER/PUBLISHER:
Clifton & Co., Bombay
UNDIVIDED BACK

General View of Durgah or Tomb of Khavaja Sahib, Ajmere

TITLE:
*General View of Durgah or Tomb of
Khavaja Sahib. Ajmere*

TITLE:
Mayo College Front View Ajmere

Zenana
in the Fort
Jodhpore

TITLE:
Zenana in the Fort Jodhpore

Baluchistan, Sindh, Rajputana & Gujarat

View of Mount Abu.

TITLE:
View of Mount Abu
PRINTER/PUBLISHER:
Printed in Saxony

The Toad Rock. Mount Abu

TITLE:
The Toad Rock. Mount Abu

Dilwara Temple. Mount Aboo.

TITLE:
Dilwara Temple. Mount Aboo

PALACE OF RANA BHEEM & PUDMUNI, OODEYPOOR.

TITLE:
Palace of Rana Bheem &
Pudmuni, Oodeypoor

PRINTER/PUBLISHER:
Printed in Germany

UNDIVIDED BACK

TITLE:
View of Chitoor

PRINTER/PUBLISHER:
Printed in Luxembourg

POSTAL USAGE:
From Bombay (India), 20 January

RUINS OF THE RUDRA MAHAL AT SIDHPORE.

TITLE:
Ruins of the Rudra Mahal at Sidhpore

PRINTER/PUBLISHER:
Printed in Germany

UNDIVIDED BACK

POSTAL USAGE:
Madras (India) to Devon (UK), February 1906

Baluchistan, Sindh, Rajputana & Gujarat

Swami Narain's Temple, Ahmedabad

TITLE:
Swami Narain's Temple, Ahmedabad

PRINTER/PUBLISHER:
Printed in Saxony

HUTHI SINGH'S TOMB, AHMEDABAD.   Clifton & Co.

TITLE:
Huthi Singh's Tomb, Ahmedabad

PRINTER/PUBLISHER:
Clifton & Co., Bombay

UNDIVIDED BACK

TITLE:
Carved Windows, Ahmedabad

Kutbudin Mosque, Ahmedabad

TITLE:
Kutbudin Mosque, Ahmedabad
PRINTER/PUBLISHER:
Printed in Saxony

TITLE:
Muhafiz Khan Mosque, Ahmedabad
PRINTER/PUBLISHER:
Clifton & Co., Bombay
UNDIVIDED BACK

5. Orphelinat d'Anand.
Weeshuis van Anand.

TITLE:
Orphelinat d'Anand - Weeshuis van Anand (Orphanage Anand)
PRINTER/PUBLISHER:
Mission East India

TITLE:
Baroda. The Gaekwars Palace

PRINTER/PUBLISHER:
Printed in Germany

PHOTOGRAPHER/ARTIST:
Bourne & Shepherd, Calcutta, Simla and Bombay

UNDIVIDED BACK

POSTAL USAGE:
Bombay (India) to London (UK), June 1906

TITLE:
State Elephants of the Gaekwar of Baroda

PRINTER/PUBLISHER:
Combridge & Co., Madras

UNDIVIDED BACK

Baluchistan, Sindh, Rajputana & Gujarat

(Copy right)   *Bird's Eye View, West–SURAT.*   *I*

TITLE:
Bird's Eye View, West - Surat
PRINTER/PUBLISHER:
Asgar G. Kapadia, Surat

JAIN TEMPLES ON GIRNAR HILLS, JUNAGADH.

TITLE:
Jain Temples on Girnar Hills, Junagadh
PRINTER/PUBLISHER:
Printed in Germany
UNDIVIDED BACK

THE FOOT OF THE SHATRUNJAYA HILLS, PALITANA.

TITLE:
The Foot of the Shatrunjaya Hills,
Palitana

PRINTER/PUBLISHER:
Printed in Germany

UNDIVIDED BACK

RAJKOTE CITY GATE.

TITLE:
Rajkote City Gate

PRINTER/PUBLISHER:
Printed in Germany

UNDIVIDED BACK

POSTAL USAGE:
c.1900

BOMBAY
GOA
&
CENTRAL
PROVINCES

शकुन्तला पत्र-लेखन   **Shakuntala writing letter**   શકુન્તલા પત્ર-લેખન

5   JOSHI BROS. *Picture Merchants*, Bazargate. Bombay

The Central Provinces (most of present-day Madhya Pradesh) passed into British hands at various times during the 19th century. Berar was assigned to the EIC by the Nizam of Hyderabad in 1853, and then leased to the British Government of India in 1903. The cotton growing on the black-soil plains of Berar and the Central Provinces countryside, and the extraction of minerals were the primary interest of the EIC/British. Railway lines brought this cotton to the textile mills of Nagpur and onward to Cotton Greens in Bombay for shipment to England.

By the end of the 19th century, Bombay emerged as the largest cotton port in the world after New Orleans, and more than half of all other imports and exports from India were passing through Bombay Customs. The city was also usually the first port of call for most Europeans sailing to India, be it photographers, artists, writers, soldiers, government officials, surveyors or travellers. As their incoming ship went around Colaba Point, the first glimpse of "Bom Bahia" or Beautiful Bay was memorable with the panorama of the city unfolding beyond the docks, surrounded by palm-covered islands and the hills of Matheran and Mahabaleshwar.

Over the centuries, diverse people from across the world have made this city their home, and during the Golden Era of picture postcards, Bombay was the largest, most populous and enterprising city of the British Empire. Considered the "Eye of India", the picture postcards of Bombay were perhaps the most varied and large in number. Looking at them now, they seem to have captured an idyllic Bombay, long gone by, newly built at that time with its spacious tree-lined avenues and hardly any vehicular traffic. It had one of the best public transport systems in India, with the first tracks for the horse-pulled tramway laid out by 1874. Early picture postcards capture trams, bullock carts and buggies ferrying people and goods around the streets of Bombay. They show the growth of the city, with the linking of the seven islands through reclamation. The construction of Sion Causeway began in 1805, of the Colaba Causeway in 1835 and of the Lady Jamsetjee Causeway to connect Mahim with Bandra in 1845. Reclamation around the harbour followed soon, primarily to meet the Indian cotton boom following the American Civil War. The Great Indian Peninsula Railway Terminus (also Victoria Terminus), the docks and Ballard Estate were built during this phase. Postcards feature the Gothic public buildings built during the years of the first Governor of Bombay, Henry Bartle Frere, with many of their embellishments designed by students of the new Sir JJ School of Arts. The clubs and hotels near the harbour that became the first short-stay homes of the Europeans feature in postcards sent back home, along with pictures of British social life, the evenings around the bandstands, local temples and sights of weekend getaways and so on. Postcards post late 1920s feature the new art-deco-styled buildings designed by European architects around Oval Maidan, Marine Drive and Malabar Hill, which became an integral part of modern Bombay's landscape.

With the increasing importance of the sea port of Bombay, the first railway of India was also commenced from here by the EIC. This rail network expanded rapidly to connect Bombay to Ahmedabad in 1863 and to Calcutta in 1870. By the time the capital of British India shifted from Calcutta to Delhi in 1911, the railway line connecting Bombay to Agra had been extended to Delhi. In fact, by 1905 itself more than 12,000 km of railway tracks open to traffic were under the Bombay Presidency to enable faster movement of passengers and goods. The Victoria Terminus Railway Station of the GIP Railway was rebuilt and reopened in 1929.

Railway advertisement of the GIP
Railway in the The Times, Weekly
Edition, 29 June 1933

The weekend excursions well known to all Mumbaikars today had become popular soon after the railway networks were established in the Bombay Presidency. Bassein, the erstwhile Portuguese city, was reached by morning trains departing from Colaba Station. W.S. Caine in his book *Picturesque India: A Handbook for European Travellers*, published in 1891, mentions interesting moonlight trips to Bassein through steam launches upto Thane, and from there by boats cruising along palm groves and islands in the late evening on the Ghodbandar River. Elephanta was popular for sightseeing and picnics, and was reached in an hour by steam launches of Thomas Cook & Sons departing from Apollo Bandar. Many a times, entire steamers were booked for private parties.

The south-eastern branch of the Great Indian Peninsula Railway from Bombay to Madras traversed the scenic Western Ghats. From Neral, a 3-foot gauge steam mountain tramway, which had commenced in 1907, climbed up 2,000 feet to Matheran, the nearest hill station to Bombay. Some travellers hiked all the way up by foot. Further on this railway line, a more powerful engine was attached at Karjat for the steep 1,850-foot ascent up the Bhore Ghat to Khandala. After gaining 1,350 feet, the train stopped for ten minutes at the Reversing Station of Khandala, featured in this postcard series, to enable the powerful engines to pass to the other end. The next station of Lonauli was the base for visiting the largest Chaitya caves of Karli. The caves were also well connected by road. Further on the railway line, the next main station was Poona (Pune), the monsoon capital of the Bombay Presidency and as such well equipped with clubs, race course, bandstands, libraries and other colonial British amenities. Roads were good between Bombay and Poona even then, and many travellers opted for the road journey via Khopoli through the picturesque ghats. Fort Purandhar, the hill sanatorium near Poona, was reached by road up the Diva Ghat.

The Southern Mahratta Railway serviced the stretch between Poona and Goa, passing through Wathar, the connecting station for the road journey to Mahabaleshwar. Sites of the old villages, such as the temple at the source of River Krishna, were depicted in postcards, besides, of course, the picturesque hilly landscapes. The train entered Goa through the Castle Rock, Dudh Sagar and Vasco da Gama stations and terminated on the quay at the Port of Mormugao. Portuguese Goa was also connected by steamers from Bombay and Calcutta, and the resulting increase in travel here increased the availability and popularity of Goa's picture postcards, published by the Portuguese.

The Great Indian Peninsula and East Indian Railways line to Calcutta went through Deolali, the halting place for troops arriving from or going back to Europe. This British army transit camp found its way into the Hobson-Jobson's Anglo-Indian colloquial dictionary as "Doolally Taap", meaning Deolali Fever or losing one's mind out of boredom and exhaustion (or mosquitoes) at the Deolali camp as a result of the heat in the heart of central India, more than 150 km from Bombay! Further, the railway journey ascended from the Konkan to the Deccan Plateau through the "Thal Ghat" mountain pass with a specially attached engine and brakes. Piparia was the station for Pachmarhi, the hill station of the Central Provinces. Jubbulpore (Jabalpur) was reached in this journey after crossing the Narmada River and was the junction for the Great Indian Peninsula and East Indian Railways. The Great Indian Peninsula Railway terminated at Nagpur, the capital of the Central Provinces.

The new Bengal-Nagpur Railway line connected Bombay to Calcutta through a much shorter route. Raigarh, that came under the British as a princely state in 1911, was further up on this railway line. Ranchi, the summer headquarters of the Government of Bihar and Orissa and an important administrative and judicial centre was well connected through the Bengal-Nagpur Railway. During the Golden Era of picture postcards, the city was a popular holiday destination from Calcutta owing to its pleasant climate and social amenities. It was reached by a narrow gauge uphill railway line.

Bombay to Gwalior and Agra:

Bombay ...	Taj Mahal Hotel	First class	—
Igatpuri ...	Dâk Bungalow	Fair	Supplies
Dhulia ...	,,	Good	,,
Ajanta Caves	,,	Fair	No supplies
Nardana ...	,,	Very bad	,,
Shirpur ...	,,	,,	,,
Palasnir ...	,,	,,	,,
Khurumpura	,,	Fair	Supplies doubtful
Khal Ghát ...	,,	Very bad	No supplies
Mhow ...	,,	Good	Supplies
Indore ...	,,	,,	,,
Dhar	,,	,,	,,
Maksi	,,	,,	,,
Sarangpur ...	,,	Poor	Supplies doubtful
Guna	,,	,,	The mess of the Central India Horse may perhaps provide supplies
Gwalior ...	Musaferkhana (now an hotel)	Good	—
Agra	Laurie's Hotel	,,	—
Fatehpur Sikri	Dâk Bungalow	Very good	Supplies

Hotels and dak bunglows en route Bombay to Agra via Gwalior listed in the book Motoring in India

Mhow and Indore, governed by the state of Holkar, were connected to the rest of the province through the narrow gauge line of the Holkar State Railway, which facilitated the ascent to the Vindhya Range. Mhow became an important military cantonment after the peace treaty between the East India Company and Maharaja Holkar in 1818.

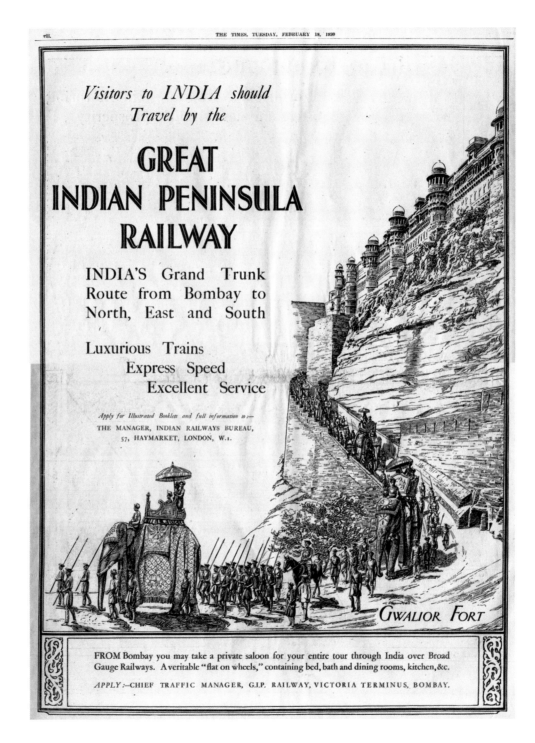

An advertisement of the Great Indian Peninsula Railway in The Times, *18 February 1930*

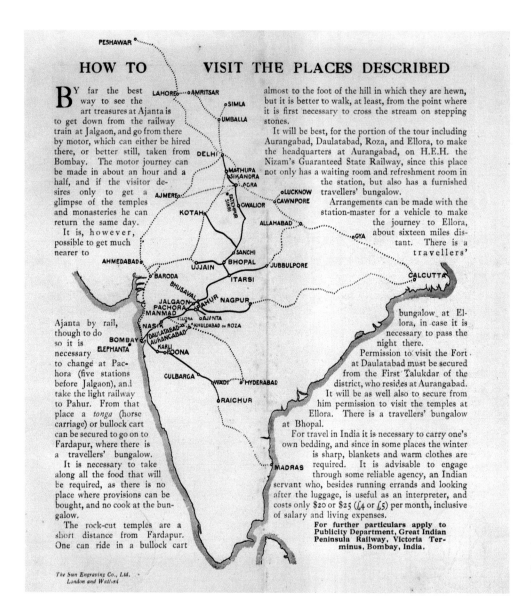

HOW TO VISIT THE PLACES DESCRIBED

BY far the best way to see the art treasures at Ajanta is to get down from the railway train at Jalgaon, and go from there by motor, which can either be hired there, or better still, taken from Bombay. The motor journey can be made in about an hour and a half, and if the visitor desires only to get a glimpse of the temples and monasteries he can return the same day.

It is, however, possible to get much nearer to Ajanta by rail, though to do so it is necessary to change at Pachora (five stations before Jalgaon), and take the light railway to Pahur. From that place a *tonga* (horse carriage) or bullock cart can be secured to go on to Fardapur, where there is a travellers' bungalow. It is necessary to take along all the food that will be required, as there is no place where provisions can be bought, and no cook at the bungalow.

The rock-cut temples are a short distance from Fardapur. One can ride in a bullock cart

almost to the foot of the hill in which they are hewn, but it is better to walk, at least, from the point where it is first necessary to cross the stream on stepping stones.

It will be best, for the portion of the tour including Aurangabad, Daulatabad, Roza, and Ellora, to make the headquarters at Aurangabad, on H.E.H. the Nizam's Guaranteed State Railway, since this place not only has a waiting room and refreshment room in the station, but also has a furnished travellers' bungalow.

Arrangements can be made with the station-master for a vehicle to make the journey to Ellora, about sixteen miles distant. There is a travellers' bungalow at Ellora, in case it is necessary to pass the night there.

Permission to visit the Fort at Daulatabad must be secured from the First Talukdar of the district, who resides at Aurangabad. It will be as well also to secure from him permission to visit the temples at Ellora. There is a travellers' bungalow at Bhopal.

For travel in India it is necessary to carry one's own bedding, and since in some places the winter is sharp, blankets and warm clothes are required. It is advisable to engage through some reliable agency, an Indian servant who, besides running errands and looking after the luggage, is useful as an interpreter, and costs only $20 or $25 ($4 or $5) per month, inclusive of salary and living expenses.

For further particulars apply to Publicity Department, Great Indian Peninsula Railway, Victoria Terminus, Bombay, India.

The Sun Engraving Co., Ltd.
London and Watford

A page from the Great Indian Peninsula Railway Brochure titled "The Road to India's Past", written by Sant Nihal Singh, c. 1920s

Jhansi became an important military cantonment after 1857 and was the central station of the Indian Midland Railway that connected Bombay with North-Western India and the other Bundelkhand cities of Bhopal, Sanchi, Datia, Gwalior and Orchha. The picture postcards of the Central Provinces capture the the region's richly decorated temples, stupas, palaces, forts and stepwells.

VIEW OF BOMBAY.

9 June '04

I am a Parsi lady of Bombay. Should you care to exchange cards with me I can send you any kind you require. I want View cards :- Mrs. F. S. Talegarkhan, Readymoney House No 2, Repean Sea Rd. Malabar Hill. Bombay

TITLE:
View of Bombay

UNDIVIDED BACK

POSTAL USAGE:
*Bombay (India) to New York
(USA), June 1904*

Gateway of India, Bombay.

Apollo Bunder and front of Taj mahal Hotel.

TITLE:
Gateway of India, Bombay

PRINTER/PUBLISHER:
Printed in Germany

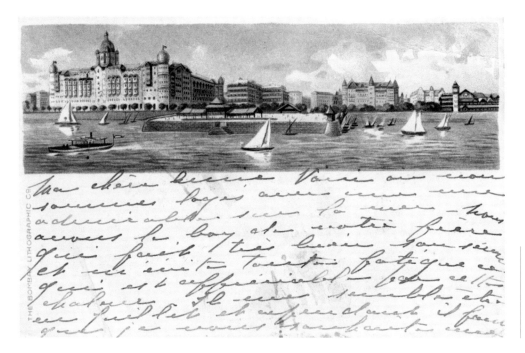

TITLE:
Taj Mahal Palace Hotel

PRINTER/PUBLISHER:
The Bombay Lithographic Co.

POSTAL USAGE:
*Bombay (India) to Paris (France),
May 1912*

THE TAJ MAHAL HOTEL AND GREENS

TITLE:
The Taj Mahal Hotel and Greens

PRINTER/PUBLISHER:
*Thacker & Co. Ltd, Bombay;
printed in England*

Royal Bombay Yacht Club.

TITLE:
Royal Bombay Yacht Club
UNDIVIDED BACK

Cuff Parade, Bombay. (Copyright.)

TITLE:
Cuff Parade, Bombay
PRINTER/PUBLISHER:
Printed in Saxony

Bombay, Goa & the Central Provinces

Souvenir of East Indies

TITLE:
Souvenir of East Indies - Bombay

UNDIVIDED BACK

Apollo Bunder, Bombay.

TITLE:
Apollo Bunder, Bombay

UNDIVIDED BACK

POSTAL USAGE:
*Bombay (India) to Hungary,
July 1905*

Government Dock and Great Western Hotel, Bombay

Bombay — Cotton dealings

The Phototype Cov. Bombay.

B. & S. Series

View of Colaba, Bombay

TITLE:
View of Colaba, Bombay

POSTAL USAGE:
*Bombay (India) to South Africa,
May 1911*

Colaba Causeway, Bombay (Copyright)

TITLE:
*Colaba Causeway,
Bombay*

PRINTER/PUBLISHER:
Printed in Saxony

The Esplanade Road and Floral Fountain, Bombay.

LOYAL JUBILEE GATHERING AT QUEENS STATUE BOMBAY

TITLE:
Loyal Jubilee Gathering at Queens Statue Bombay

PRINTER/PUBLISHER:
Printed in Germany

UNDIVIDED BACK

POSTAL USAGE:
Poona (India) to Edinburgh (UK), September 1904

Statue of Lord Reay, Bombay.

TITLE:
Statue of Lord Reay, Bombay

PRINTER/PUBLISHER:
Printed in Germany

King Edward's Statue. Bombay

TITLE:
King Edward's Statue, Bombay

TITLE:
Town Hall, Bombay

PRINTER/PUBLISHER:
Clifton & Co., Bombay

UNDIVIDED BACK

POSTAL USAGE:
Bombay (India) to Prague (Czech Republic), May 1903

TITLE:
Elphinstone Circle, Bombay

PRINTER/PUBLISHER:
Printed in Germany

UNDIVIDED BACK

POSTAL USAGE:
Bombay (India) to Port Said (Egypt), December 1908

The Bombay Club.

The Phototype Coy. Bombay.

TITLE:
The Bombay Club

PRINTER/PUBLISHER:
The Phototype Co., Bombay

UNDIVIDED BACK

Best wishes for a Happy Christmas and Prosperous new Year. We were so sorry not to have seen you before leaving but our time was so short Philip sends his special love to you and regrets not being

The Police Head-Quarters. Bombay *with you for Boxing Day. H. J.*

TITLE:
The Police Head-Quarters, Bombay

PRINTER/PUBLISHER:
D.B. Taraporevala & Sons, Bombay

UNDIVIDED BACK

POSTAL USAGE:
Bombay (India) to London (UK), December 1906

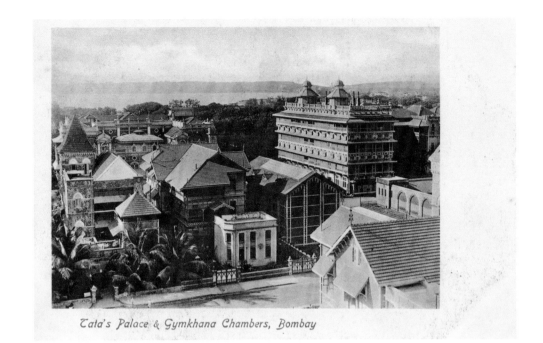

Tata's Palace & Gymkhana Chambers, Bombay

TITLE:
*Tata's Palace & Gymkhana
Chambers, Bombay*

PRINTER/PUBLISHER:
*D.B. Taraporevala & Sons,
Bombay; printed in Germany*

UNDIVIDED BACK

View from Watson's Hotel, Bombay.

TITLE:
View from Watson's Hotel, Bombay

UNDIVIDED BACK

POSTAL USAGE:
*Bombay (India) to New York
(USA), October 1904*

THE MUSEUM AND INSTITUTE OF SCIENCE, BOMBAY

A. R. Haseler. Copyright

TITLE:
The Museum and Institute of Science, Bombay

PRINTER/PUBLISHER:
Thacker & Co. Ltd, Bombay; printed in England

PHOTOGRAPHER/ARTIST:
A.R. Haselar

POSTAL USAGE:
Bombay (India) to Prague (Czech Republic), February 1930

Cocoanut Festival, Bombay.

TITLE:
Cocoanut Festival, Bombay

UNDIVIDED BACK

POSTAL USAGE:
Philippines to Ohio (USA), February 1907

TITLE:
Die Tatschali - Line in Bombay

PRINTER/PUBLISHER:
Joseph Hoffmann

PHOTOGRAPHER/ARTIST:
Joseph Hoffmann (Jos Heim)

UNDIVIDED BACK

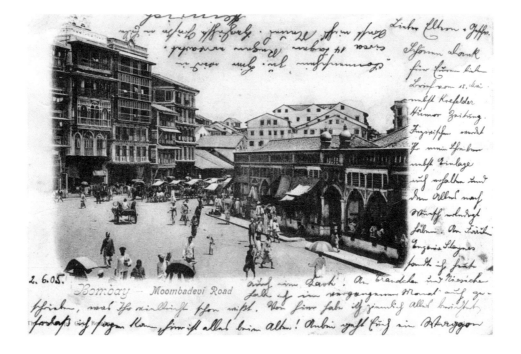

TITLE:
Bombay - Moombadevi Road

PRINTER/PUBLISHER:
Thacker & Co. Ltd, Bombay

UNDIVIDED BACK

POSTAL USAGE:
Bombay (India) to Krefeld (Germany), June 1905

Old
Hunuman
Street,
Bombay.

TITLE:
Old Hunuman Street, Bombay

PRINTER/PUBLISHER:
Printed in Germany

Crawford Market,
Bombay

TITLE:
Crawford Market, Bombay

POSTAL USAGE:
India to Graz (Austria), April 1912

Picturesque India

Girgaum Back Road, Bombay

TITLE:
Girgaum Back Road, Bombay
PRINTER/PUBLISHER:
Printed in Saxony

PARSEE STATUE, BYCULLA, BOMBAY

TITLE:
Parsee Statue, Byculla, Bombay
PRINTER/PUBLISHER:
*Thacker & Co. Ltd, Bombay;
printed in England*
POSTAL USAGE:
*India to Czech Republic,
February 1925*

Byculla Club Bombay

TITLE:
Byculla Club Bombay

PRINTER/PUBLISHER:
*D.B. Taraporevala & Sons,
Bombay; printed in Germany*

UNDIVIDED BACK

THE CENTRAL STATION. B.B. AND C.I. RAILWAY

17ᵗʰ Jany. 1935

TITLE:
*The Central Station. B.B. and
C.I. Railway*

PRINTER/PUBLISHER:
*Thacker & Co. Ltd, Bombay;
printed in England*

ROYAL MAIL LEAVING BOMBAY, GREAT INDIAN PENINSULA RY.

TITLE:
View from Malabar Hill, Bombay

PRINTER/PUBLISHER:
Clifton & Co., Bombay

UNDIVIDED BACK

POSTAL USAGE:
Bombay (India) to Prague (Czech Republic), September 1905

TITLE:
Malabar Hill, Bombay

POSTAL USAGE:
Bombay (India) to Czech Republic, March 1921

H.E. THE GOVERNOR OF BOMBAY DRIVING THROUGH WALKESHWAR ROAD, BOMBAY.

TITLE:
H.E. The Governor of Bombay Driving Through Walkeshwar Road, Bombay

PRINTER/PUBLISHER:
Printed in Germany

UNDIVIDED BACK

POSTAL USAGE:
Ratnagiri (India) to England (UK), May 1905

Parsee Tower of Silence. Bombay.

TITLE:
Parsee Tower of Silence. Bombay

PRINTER/PUBLISHER:
Printed in Germany

GANGA TANK. WALKESHWAR. BOMBAY.

TITLE:
Ganga Tank, Walkeshwar, Bombay

PRINTER/PUBLISHER:
Printed in Germany

UNDIVIDED BACK

Mahalakshmi Temple, Bombay

TITLE:
Mahalakshmi Temple, Bombay

PRINTER/PUBLISHER:
*P.S. Joshi, Oriental Publishing
House, Bombay; printed in Germany*

TITLE:
Dhobie Ghat at Mahalakshmi

TITLE:
A Village Scene, Matunga, Bombay

PRINTER/PUBLISHER:
Printed in Germany

POSTAL USAGE:
From Bombay (India)

Old Fort at Mahim, Bombay (Copyright).

Sea

TITLE:
Old Fort at Mahim, Bombay

PRINTER/PUBLISHER:
Printed in Germany

View from Bandora Point

TITLE:
View from Bandora Point

PRINTER/PUBLISHER:
The Phototype Co., Bombay;
printed in Luxembourg

Bombay, Goa & the Central Provinces

217

Powai Lake off Bombay.

TITLE:
Powai Lake off Bombay
PRINTER/PUBLISHER:
Thacker & Co. Ltd, Bombay

HINDU TEMPLE BASSEIN

TITLE:
Hindu Temple, Bassein
PRINTER/PUBLISHER:
*Clifton & Co., Bombay;
printed in Belgium*

TITLE:
Souvenir of East Indies -
Buddhistentempel Elefanta
(Buddhist temple, Elephanta)

PRINTER/PUBLISHER:
Weltreise Verlag Compagnie Comet,
Fr. Th & Co., Dresden

UNDIVIDED BACK

POSTAL USAGE:
Bombay (India) to Bautzen
(Germany), January 1904

Buddhistentempel Elefanta.

Souvenir of East Indies

TITLE:
View from Louisa Point, Matheran

PRINTER/PUBLISHER:
Printed in Germany

UNDIVIDED BACK

VIEW FROM LOUISA POINT, MATHERAN.

The Reversing Station, Khandalla.

TITLE:
The Reversing Station, Khandalla

PRINTER/PUBLISHER:
Printed in Germany

View of Khandalla. *" S. S. Sangale ." 8|10|05*

A place about 6 miles out from Bombay. Looks all right on a picture post cards. "Adelboslett."

TITLE:
View of Khandalla

UNDIVIDED BACK

POSTAL USAGE:
*Bombay (India) to Surrey (UK),
October 1905*

Karli Cave

TITLE:
Karli Cave

PRINTER/PUBLISHER:
Printed in Saxony

TITLE:
Poona Railway Station

PRINTER/PUBLISHER:
The Commercial Printing Works,
Poona; printed in England

The Grand Stand Race Course, Poona

TITLE:
The Grand Stand Race
Course, Poona

PRINTER/PUBLISHER:
Printed in Saxony

The Club of Western India, Poona.

TITLE:
The Club of Western India, Poona

UNDIVIDED BACK

POSTAL USAGE:
India to Bohemia (Czech Republic),
October 1905

Rosherville, Kirkee Boat Club, Poona.

TITLE:
Rosherville, Kirkee Boat Club, Poona

PRINTER/PUBLISHER:
Printed in Saxony

TITLE:
The Connaught Hotel Poona

PHOTOGRAPHER /ARTIST:
Souvenir Photo Co., Poona

POSTAL USAGE:
Poona (India) to Prostejov (Czech Republic), November 1931

TITLE:
Reay Market, Poona

PRINTER/PUBLISHER:
Printed in Saxony

TITLE:
Arsenal Road, Poona

PRINTER/PUBLISHER:
*Ahmed Kasim & Co., Poona;
printed in Saxony*

Bombay, Goa & the Central Provinces

225

Prisoners making Cane Chairs, Yarrowda Jail.

TITLE:
*Prisoners making Cane Chairs,
Yarrowda Jail*

PRINTER/PUBLISHER:
Printed in Saxony

Government House, Ganeshkhind.

Clifton & Co., Bombay.

TITLE:
Government House, Ganeshkhind

PRINTER/PUBLISHER:
Clifton & Co., Bombay

UNDIVIDED BACK

Harris Bridge & River, Poona

TITLE:
Harris Bridge & River, Poona

PRINTER/PUBLISHER:
Printed in Saxony

POSTAL USAGE:
c. 1920s

Dolkar's Bridge, Poona

TITLE:
Dolkar's Bridge, Poona

PRINTER/PUBLISHER:
Printed in Saxony

POSTAL USAGE:
c. 1920s

Fort Purandhar, near Poona.

New Forest Ride Road, Mahabaleshwar.

TITLE:
Fort Purandhar, near Poona

PRINTER/PUBLISHER:
Ahmed Kasim & Co., Poona;
printed in Saxony

TITLE:
New Forest Ride Road,
Mahabaleshwar

PRINTER/PUBLISHER:
Ali Mahomed Fazal, Bombay;
printed in Saxony

PHOTOGRAPHER/ARTIST:
Devare

UNDIVIDED BACK

POSTAL USAGE:
Hyderabad (India) to Austria,
April 1907

TITLE:
Panorama View of Mahabhleshwar

Cows mouth old Mahableshwar

TITLE:
Cows Mouth Old Mahableshwar

PRINTER/PUBLISHER:
*Dias & Co., Mahableshwar;
printed in Germany*

Mormugão - India Portugesa - Quebra-mar visto do poente.

TITLE:
Mormugao - India Portugesa - Quebra-mar visto do poente

PRINTER/PUBLISHER:
Edicao de Christovam Fernandes, Nova Goa

VIEW OF MARMAGOA PORT GÔA.
VISTA DO PORTO DE MORMUGÃO. GÔA.

TITLE:
View of Marmagoa Port Goa

PHOTOGRAPHER/ARTIST:
Souza & Paul Fotografos, Nova Goa

CHURCH OF PANGIM. (NOVA - GÔA).
IGREJA DE PANGIM. (NOVA - GÔA).

Dona Paula - India Portugesa - Caes.

TITLE:
Dona Paula - India Portugesa - Caes

PRINTER/PUBLISHER:
*Edicao de Christovam Fernandes,
Nova Goa*

VIEW OF PANGIM. HARBOUR. (NOVA-GÔA).
VISTA DO PORTO DE PANGIM. (NOVA-GÔA).

TITLE:
*View of Pangim. Harbour.
(Nova - Goa)*

PHOTOGRAPHER/ARTIST:
*Souza & Paul Fotografos,
Nova Goa*

VIEW OF FERRY STEAMER PIER, PANGIM. (NOVA - GÔA).
VISTA DOS CAES DE NAVEGACAS FLUVIAL PANGIM. (NOVA - GÔA).

TITLE:
View of Ferry Steamer Pier, Pangim. (Nova - Goa)

PHOTOGRAPHER/ARTIST:
Souza & Paul Fotografos, Nova Goa

Deolali.

TITLE:
Deolali

PRINTER/PUBLISHER:
Printed in Saxony

TITLE:
Little Fall Pachmarhi
UNDIVIDED BACK

SADAR BAZAR, JUBBULPORE.

TITLE:
Sadar Bazar, Jubbulpore

TOWN HALL, JUBBULPORE.   No. 34.

TITLE:
Town Hall Jubbulpore

PRINTER/PUBLISHER:
G.K. Husain & Co., Jubbulpore

POSTAL USAGE:
India to Birmingham (UK)

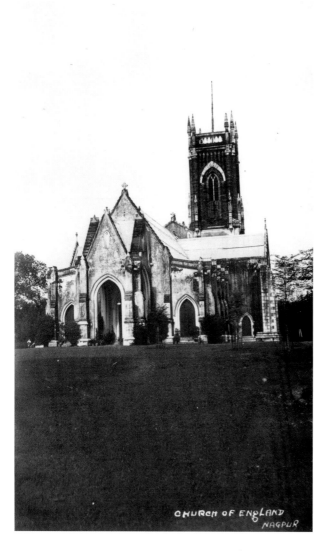

TITLE:
Church of England, Nagpur

TITLE:
Raigarh Castle

PRINTER/PUBLISHER:
Printed in Luxembourg

Strasse in Ranchi.

TITLE:
Strasse in Ranchi
UNDIVIDED BACK

British Infantry Line, Mhow

TITLE:
British Infantry Line, Mhow
PRINTER/PUBLISHER:
Printed in Bavaria

VIEW ON THE INDORE RIVER.

TITLE:
View on the Indore River
PRINTER/PUBLISHER:
Raphael Tuck & Sons, London
UNDIVIDED BACK
POSTAL USAGE:
*Bombay (India) to Bohemia
(Czech Republic)*

TITLE:
Dhobie Bridge - Jhansi

PRINTER/PUBLISHER:
Moorli Dhur & Sons, Ambala;
printed in Germany

Club Gardens — Jhansi.

TITLE:
Club Gardens - Jhansi

PRINTER/PUBLISHER:
Moorli Dhur & Sons, Ambala;
printed in Germany

Bombay, Goa & the Central Provinces

Moti Mehel Bhopal

View of Sanchi Tope Bhopal

New Electric Alijah Durbar Press, Gwalior.

TITLE:
Gwalior Fort

PRINTER/PUBLISHER:
Clifton & Co., Bombay

UNDIVIDED BACK

POSTAL USAGE:
*Within Edinburgh (UK),
January 1904*

TITLE:
*Ancient Buddhist
Temple, Gwalior*

PRINTER/PUBLISHER:
Clifton & Co, Bombay

UNDIVIDED BACK

OLD MAUSOLEUMS, ORCHA.

TITLE:
Old Mausoleums, Orcha
UNDIVIDED BACK

BOMBAY-POONA MAIL
GREAT INDIAN PENINSULA RLY

TITLE:
Bombay-Poona Mail. Great Indian Peninsula Rly

PRINTER/PUBLISHER:
Raphael Tuck & Sons; printed in England

Bombay, Goa & the Central Provinces

BENGAL
DARJEELING
SIKKIM
ASSAM
BIHAR
&
ORISSA

INDIA
HALF ANNA

La Poste aux Indes Anglaises

The Bengal Presidency was established in 1765, with Calcutta functioning as its capital between 1772 and 1911 and Darjeeling as the summer capital. As the capital, Calcutta became the first economic, socio-cultural and educational hub of the British Raj on one hand, and the hotbed of the Indian Nationalist Movement and the Bengal Renaissance on the other. The first of the EIC Indologists arrived here, and Sir William Jones had established the Asiatic Society by 1784. The Imperial (Indian) Museum was born out of the Asiatic Society in the 1800s. The Fort William College was also established in the year 1800, and the focus of all these institutions was Oriental cultural and religious studies and philology. Photographers working in the Bengal Presidency travelled along with archaeologists and surveyors to photograph heritage sites and to photo-document the antiquities and other art objects that these institutions acquired over time.

The Christmas and New Year festivities of Calcutta were the most sought after events for the British, complete with annual races, charitable fetes, drawing room balls and garden parties. Officers stationed across the country made sure they reached Calcutta in time during the Christmas holidays to partake in the celebrations. In those days, if you didn't plan ahead, it was hard to even find a decent hotel room during this high season. The Calcutta Christmas and New Year festivities feature abundantly in the postcards and books on British social life in

FACING PAGE:

Postcard titled "La Poste aux Indes Anglaises"

India during the 19th and 20th centuries, and in other written accounts, sketches and photographs as well.

Some of the oldest, postally used coloured lithographic art postcards and even black-and-white photographic postcards of India are those of Calcutta city. The postcards of this first capital of the Empire, so likened to London, show the grandeur of the sprawling government buildings built by the British, beginning with the creation of Fort William in 1781. Postcards of streets and esplanades filled with trams, rickshaws and horse carriages, the busy port along the Hooghly and devotees offering their prayers at the temples of Kalighat were the first to be sent out to friends and family halfway across the world. Needless to say, the two favourites of the Europeans during their visits to Calcutta, the Great Eastern Hotel and Grand Hotel, feature in numerous picture postcards of the city.

From Calcutta, popular river excursions via Barrackpore on the Hooghly were to destinations such as the erstwhile Portuguese settlement of Bandel, where one of the oldest churches was built in 1599; to Chandernagore, where the French settled in 1673; and to Serampore, formerly known as the Danish settlement of "Fredericksnagar". Serampore is best known for the oldest printing press in Bengal; their very first publication in the year 1778 was the Orientalist Nathaniel Brassey Halhed's *A Grammar of the Bengal Language*.

The mountain journey from Calcutta to the summer capital Darjeeling and the neighbouring cantonment of Jallapahar was one of the oldest and most celebrated during the British Raj. It had evolved from a 98-hour journey done in "dak gharries" or mail carriages and *tonga*s to a much faster transit facilitated by the broad guage Eastern Bengal Railway connecting Calcutta to Siliguri in 1878, and the subsequent 8-hour journey from Siliguri to Darjeeling facilitated by the narrow gauge Darjeeling Himalayan Railway, completed in 1881. The locomotives were manufactured at Sharp, Stewart & Co. in Manchester, with funds entirely raised in India for the first time.

Hotels and dak bungalows en route Delhi to Calcutta listed in the book Motoring in India: A Guide for the Tourist and Resident *by Charles Watney and Mrs Herbert Lloyd, published by Car Illustrated Ltd, London, 1909*

Now a Mountain Railways of India World Heritage Site, this very first hill railway journey in India, recreated largely along the old Hill Cart Road, contained five loops and many Z reverses, rising to a maximum height of 7,000 feet. Starting early in the morning from Siliguri, the narrow gauge railway passed through Sookna, halted for breakfast at Teendaria and continued to Kurseong, the speed not permitted to exceed 16 miles an hour. Best views of the scenery and the highest peaks of the Himalayan ranges, including Mount Everest, were from the front seats of the open carriages built to seat six passengers. Travel guides advised passengers to wear spectacles or veils to protect from the dust and blacks emitted by the engine! At that time, a fair amount of trade of goods, most importantly indigo, flourished between Darjeeling and Tibet through the new road built across Sikkim.

In 1905, with the partition of Bengal, the provincial government of Assam and Eastern Bengal, or Bangladesh of today, shifted to Dacca (Dhaka) in winter and to Shillong, the military cantonment, in the summer. The Bengal-Assam Railway connected Calcutta to Badarpur and Gauhati (Guwahati) and a very good road connection was also built, with numerous dak bungalows along the way from Gauhati to Shillong.

This expansion eastward from Calcutta was driven primarily by the EIC's commercial interests in tea. The first tea gardens were opened in Darjeeling in 1856 and, by the early 1900s, Assam had 900 tea gardens across Surma Valley, Silchar, Sylhet and Julpaigari (Jalpaiguri), producing 200 million pounds of tea. Trips to tea gardens were popular and arranged through the Calcutta or London agents of the tea estates. There are many postcards of the Darjeeling region during this period between 1890 to 1947, however, there are very few picture postcards of the states of Assam, Tripura and other parts of Bengal and the North-East region of modern India. The few picture postcards of this region that came into circulation were mostly of European missionaries operating from the Shillong region.

With Bihar coming under the EIC after the Battle of Buxar in 1764, Bankipore functioned as the administrative centre of the Patna division till the early 20th century. According to the Indologist William Jones, Bankipore was situated on the site of ancient Patliputra, which, as described by Megasthenes, was the confluence of the rivers Ganga and Sone. The confluence has moved further upstream since. Colonial-era buildings such as the Civil Court and District Collectorate feature in picture postcards of Bankipore. Bankipore and the nearby garrison town of Dinapore (Danapur) were connected to Calcutta through the East Indian Railway. The British India Government exercised virtual monopoly over the entire opium production in Bengal and Bihar, with this region's opium being the largest source of income for the EIC at one time. Picture postcards of this region also feature the holy sights of Gaya and Bodh Gaya, which were connected to Bankipore by the Patna-Gaya Railway.

The development of the stretch southwards to Orissa (Odisha) was motivated by a desire to connect Calcutta Presidency to Madras Presidency via the port town

RIGHT:
Railway advertisement in The
Times, *Weekly Edition (Special
India Colour Number), London,
29 June 1933*

EXTREME RIGHT:
*A detailed map of the East
Indian Railway published in
the EIR Souvenir Brochure
titled "A trip through the land of
sunshine and surprise over the
EIR", 1912*

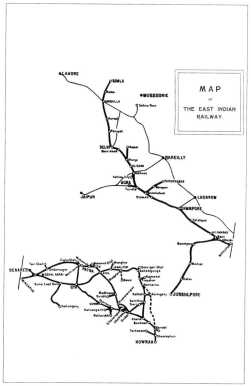

Waltair (Vizagapatam or Vishakapatnam) on the Coromandel Coast. The journey from Calcutta to Madras, skirting the Coromandel Coast, took over 40 hours and was facilitated by the Bengal-Nagpur Railway. The railway line passed through Bihar, taking travellers to Bhubaneswar, the city of temples, and Cuttack, the seat of the government of Orissa and important commercially and militarily since it lay at the centre of Orissa's system of canals. Docks were built at Cuttack to provide warehouses for goods moving across the Mahanadi and through other canals in Orissa and the Central Provinces right upto Raipur.

Since early times, sailors approaching India's eastern coast were navigated by the "White Pagoda" of Jagannath Puri and the "Black Pagoda" of Konark to its north, both visible from miles away. During the Golden Era of picture postcards, travellers also caught the glimpse of the temples of Bhubaneswar and Puri as the train approached these cities. In 1912, when the temple idols at Jagannath Temple were renewed (an event occurring every 36 years), the Bengal-Nagpur Railway had recorded bringing 1,60,000 pilgrims to Puri out of the 3,00,000 present in the city during the festival.

The simplified name of this holy city as "Puri" was popularised during the British era, replacing its ancient name of "Sri Kshetra". Since the European photographers and artists were not allowed inside the Jagannath Temple, postcards capture the temple exteriors and the wide and famous Car Street or Bara Danda Street, especially during the annual "Rath" or Car Festival. Sketches, paintings, postcards and posters of the "Car Festival at Puri", with its colour, sounds, excitement and devotion, became one of the most well-known images of festivals and celebration from India the world over, even though, at times, as the corrupted "Juggernaut". Puri, being an overnight train ride from Calcutta with the Bengal-Nagpur Railway, became a popular seaside destination with its refreshing sea breeze offering respite to the Europeans from the humid weather of Calcutta. Over time, many seaside private bungalows and hotels came up. Steamers occasionally called at Puri at that time though there wasn't a proper landing place or shelter as can be seen from the postcards. A rare picture postcard, posted in 1914 to Germany, features the mountainous adivasi region of Koraput, popular for its hill stations with picturesque valleys and waterfalls.

TITLE:
Calcutta

PRINTER/PUBLISHER:
*W. Rossler, Calcutta;
printed in Austria*

UNDIVIDED BACK

POSTAL USAGE:
*Calcutta (India) to Vienna
(Austria), October 1897*

View of the Hooghly from the High Court, Calcutta.

TITLE:
*View of the Hooghly from the High
Court, Calcutta*

The River showing Jetties and Howrah Bridge.   Calcutta.

7027.   Photo Johnston & Hoffmann.

Aylesford at high tide

TITLE:
The River showing Jetties and Howrah Bridge. Calcutta

PHOTOGRAPHER/ARTIST:
Johnston & Hoffmann

UNDIVIDED BACK

POSTAL USAGE:
Calcutta (India) to Kent (UK), April 1904

SHIPPING ON THE HOOGHLY — CALCUTTA.

Thacker, Spink & Co., Calcutta.

Calcutta 25/12/02 My dear Dorothy — Thank you very much for your charming card & for the good wishes it contains Your affect Uncle marlyn

TITLE:
Shipping on the Hooghly - Calcutta

PRINTER/PUBLISHER:
Thacker, Spink & Co., Calcutta

UNDIVIDED BACK

POSTAL USAGE:
Calcutta (India) to London (UK), December 1902

Picturesque India

254

TITLE:
Calcutta

PRINTER/PUBLISHER:
*Orbis Publishing House,
Czech Republic*

PHOTOGRAPHER/ARTIST:
Hbeshke

UNDIVIDED BACK

POSTAL USAGE:
*Calcutta (India) to Brno
(Czech Republic), July 1900*

TITLE:
Shipping in Hooghly, Calcutta

PRINTER/PUBLISHER:
Clifton & Co., Bombay

UNDIVIDED BACK

POSTAL USAGE:
*Calcutta (India) to Prague (Czech
Republic), December 1902*

SHIPPING IN HOOGHLY, CALCUTTA.

Shipping on the Hooghly, Calcutta.

Photo Johnston & Hoffmann

TITLE:
Shipping on the Hooghly, Calcutta

PHOTOGRAPHER/ARTIST:
Johnston & Hoffmann

POSTAL USAGE:
Calcutta (India) to Marseilles (France), February 1911

CALCUTTA
Pontoon Bridge over the Hooghly

Thacker, Spink & Co., Calcutta.

TITLE:
Calcutta - Pontoon Bridge over the Hooghly

PRINTER/PUBLISHER:
Thacker, Spink & Co., Calcutta

UNDIVIDED BACK

POSTAL USAGE:
Within Calcutta (India), January 1902

THE STRAND, CALCUTTA. *2/7.04* Clifton & Co.

TITLE:
The Strand, Calcutta

PRINTER/PUBLISHER:
Clifton & Co., Bombay

UNDIVIDED BACK

POSTAL USAGE:
Calcutta (India) to Hanover (Germany), July 1904

PLASSEY GATE FORT WILLIAM CALCUTTA.

TITLE:
Plassey Gate Fort William Calcutta

PRINTER/PUBLISHER:
D. Macropolo & Co., Calcutta; printed in Germany

POSTAL USAGE:
Lahore (Pakistan) to Prague (Czech Republic), January 1912

Fort William, Calcutta.

CALCUTTA. INTERIOR VIEW FORT WILLIAM.

CALCUTTA. ROYAL BARRACK FORT WILLIAM.

TITLE:
*Calcutta. Royal Barrack,
Fort William*

PRINTER/PUBLISHER:
D. Macropolo & Co., Calcutta

Hussars Barracks, Guard Room.

TITLE:
Hussars Barracks, Guard Room

PRINTER/PUBLISHER:
*English Emporium, Bangalore;
printed in England by Raphael Tuck
& Sons, London*

CALCUTTA.

Mnoho políbení a pozdravů

Čáslav dne 30 března. *od Její Irmy.*

TITLE:
Calcutta

PRINTER/PUBLISHER:
Kosmos, Budapest

UNDIVIDED BACK

POSTAL USAGE:
Caslav (Czech Republic) to Turnau (Austria), November 1899

Clive Street at Midday, Calcutta

TITLE:
Clive Street at Midday, Calcutta

PRINTER/PUBLISHER:
Thartmann; printed in Saxony

TITLE:
Chowringhee and Tram Terminus. Calcutta

PRINTER/PUBLISHER:
Raphael Tuck & Sons, London; printed in England

TITLE:
Calcutta - Chowringhee

PRINTER/PUBLISHER:
Raphael Tuck & Sons, London; processed in Germany

Bengal, Darjeeling, Sikkim, Assam, Bihar & Orissa

VIEW FROM CHOWRINGHEE — CALCUTTA.   No. 3.

TITLE:
View from Chowringhee - Calcutta

PRINTER/PUBLISHER:
D.A. Ahuja, Rangoon;
printed in Germany

POSTAL USAGE:
Calcutta (India) to Prague (Czech
Republic), March 1911

Grand Hotel, Chowringhee Road, Calcutta.

TITLE:
Grand Hotel, Chowringhee
Road, Calcutta

PRINTER/PUBLISHER:
Nissim Bros, Calcutta

TITLE:
Calcutta - Great Eastern Hotel
PRINTER/PUBLISHER:
Art Union, Calcutta

Bengal, Darjeeling, Sikkim, Assam, Bihar & Orissa

TITLE:
The Great Eastern Hotel. Calcutta

PRINTER/PUBLISHER:
W. Newman & Co. Ltd, Calcutta

POSTAL USAGE:
Calcutta (India) to Berne (Switzerland), February 1924

Old Court House Street. CALCUTTA.

TITLE:
Old Court House Street. Calcutta

UNDIVIDED BACK

Calcutta,
Old Court House Street.

339 Published by
Ad. Wiesenfeld, Hamburg.

TITLE:
Calcutta. Old Court House Street

PRINTER/PUBLISHER:
Ad. Wiesenfeld, Hamburg

UNDIVIDED BACK

POSTAL USAGE:
Calcutta (India) to Brno (Czech Republic), May 1900

CALCUTTA Old Court House Street

TITLE:
Calcutta - Old Court House Street

PRINTER/PUBLISHER:
Thacker, Spink & Co., Calcutta

UNDIVIDED BACK

POSTAL USAGE:
Calcutta (India) to Austria, January 1902

CALCUTTA _ Central Telegraph Office & Old Court House St.

TITLE:
Calcutta - Central Telegraph Office
& Old Court House St.

PRINTER/PUBLISHER:
The Oriental Commercial
Bureau, Calcutta

Old Court House Street, Calcutta.

TITLE:
Old Court House Street, Calcutta

PRINTER/PUBLISHER:
Raphael Tuck & Sons, London;
printed in England

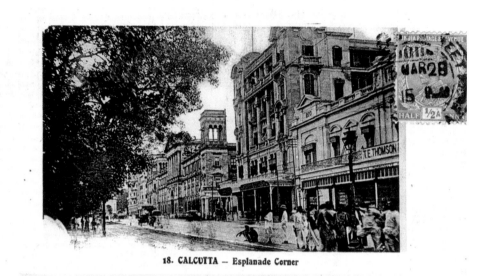

18. CALCUTTA — Esplanade Corner

TITLE:
Calcutta - Esplanade Corner

PRINTER/PUBLISHER:
Art Union, Calcutta

POSTAL USAGE:
March 1928

Esplanade Row, east — Calcutta

TITLE:
Esplanade Row, East - Calcutta

PRINTER/PUBLISHER:
Printed in Saxony

TITLE:
Municipal Market, Calcutta

PRINTER/PUBLISHER:
*Raphael Tuck & Sons, London;
printed in England*

BABU BADRIDAS'S JAIN TEMPLE, CALCUTTA

TITLE:
*Babu Badridas's Jain
Temple, Calcutta*

PRINTER/PUBLISHER:
Printed in Germany

UNDIVIDED BACK

POSTAL USAGE:
*Ahmedabad (India) to Bristol
(UK), April 1905*

TITLE:
Calcutta - Kalighat

PRINTER/PUBLISHER:
*W. Rossler, Calcutta;
printed in Austria*

UNDIVIDED BACK

TITLE:
*Heiliger Badeplatz am Hughly,
Calcutta (Holy Bathing
Place on the River Hooghly)*

PRINTER/PUBLISHER:
Verlag von L. Holub, Freiheit

UNDIVIDED BACK

POSTAL USAGE:
*Prachatice (Czech Republic) to
Pardubice (Czech Republic),
July 1901*

Bengal, Darjeeling, Sikkim, Assam, Bihar & Orissa

269

MOSQUE TALLYGUNGE. CALCUTTA.

A. H. Perris, Calcutta.

Dharumtollah Street, Calcutta.

No. 108

The Bengal Secretariat, Calcutta.

Made in Austria for W. RÖSSLER, CALCUTTA.

HIGHCOURT.   CALCUTTA. *30. I. 02.* GOVERNMENT HOUSE.

View of Writers
Buildings.
Calcutta.

7030. Photo Johnston & Hoffmann.

TITLE:
View of Writers Buildings. Calcutta

PHOTOGRAPHER/ARTIST:
Johnston & Hoffmann

UNDIVIDED BACK

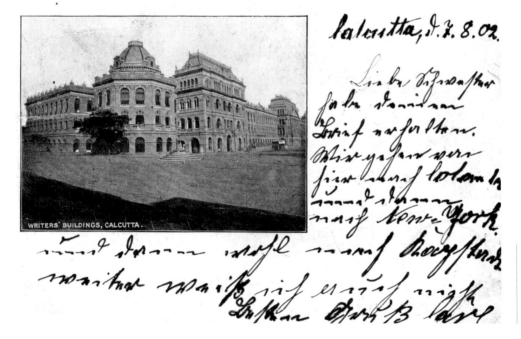

WRITERS' BUILDINGS, CALCUTTA.

TITLE:
Writers' Buildings. Calcutta

UNDIVIDED BACK

POSTAL USAGE:
*Calcutta (India) to Memel or
Klaipeda (Lithuania), August 1902*

Bank of Bengal. — CALCUTTA   4167

TITLE:
Bank of Bengal. Calcutta

PRINTER/PUBLISHER:
Printed in Austria

POSTAL USAGE:
India to Brazil, September 1906

Dalhousie Square, Calcutta.

TITLE:
Dalhousie Square, Calcutta

POSTAL USAGE:
*Calcutta (India) to Marseilles
(France), December 1910*

Sudder street from top of Museum — CALCUTTA   S. D. M. 4184

TITLE:
Sudder street from top of Museum - Calcutta
PRINTER/PUBLISHER:
Printed in Austria

R. C. Cathedral.   Chandernagore.

TITLE:
R. C. Cathedral. Chandernagore
PRINTER/PUBLISHER:
Printed in Saxony

Souvenir of East Indies ⁷⁸

Sirampore

TITLE:
Souvenir of East Indies - Sirampore

PRINTER/PUBLISHER:
Weltreise Verlag Compagnie Comet,
Fr. Th & Co., Dresden

UNDIVIDED BACK

KURSEONG VIEW OF ST HELEN'S AND MONTEVIOT VILLA. D.207

TITLE:
Kurseong View of St Helen's and
Monteviot Villa

PRINTER/PUBLISHER:
D. Macropolo & Co., Calcutta;
printed in Germany

VIEW OF KURSEONG FROM DOWHILL ROAD.

TITLE:
View of Kurseong from Dowhill Road

PRINTER/PUBLISHER:
G. C. Banerjee & Sons, Kurseong; printed in Germany

POSTAL USAGE:
Kurseong (India) to Calcutta (India), June 1911

TITLE:
Darjeeling Railway

PRINTER/PUBLISHER:
Clifton & Co., Bombay

UNDIVIDED BACK

DOUBLE LOOP ON DARJEELING—HIMALAYAN RAILWAY.

TITLE:
Double loop on Darjeeling -
Himalayan Railway

PRINTER/PUBLISHER:
Thacker, Spink & Co., Calcutta

UNDIVIDED BACK

POSTAL USAGE:
Calcutta (India) to Vienna
(Austria), March 1903

TITLE:
On reverse side: De Aartsbisschop
van Calcutta op reis door de wildernis
(The Archbishop of Calcutta on a
journey through the wilderness)

PRINTER/PUBLISHER:
Printed in Belgium

POSTAL USAGE:
Within Belgium, May 1928

VIEW FROM POST OFFICE ROAD

G. SINGH
DARJEELING

TITLE:
View from Post Office Road

PHOTOGRAPHER/ARTIST:
G. Singh, Darjeeling

POSTAL USAGE:
*Darjeeling (India) to Gossau
(Switzerland), February 1951*

JUBELI SANITARIUM AND ROSE BANK. DARJEELING.

TITLE:
*Jubeli Sanitarium and
Rose Bank - Darjeeling*

PRINTER/PUBLISHER:
*G. C. Banerjee & Sons, Kurseong;
printed in Germany*

Government House-Darjeeling

TITLE:
Government House - Darjeeling
PRINTER/PUBLISHER:
Printed in Germany

DARJEELING. THE MALL LOOKING TOWARDS WOODLANDS.

TITLE:
Darjeeling. The Mall looking towards Woodlands
PRINTER/PUBLISHER:
D. Macropolo & Co., Calcutta; printed in Germany

TITLE:
Darjeeling - A market on Sunday Morning

PRINTER/PUBLISHER:
Printed in Germany

TITLE:
Clouds at Darjeeling
PRINTER/PUBLISHER:
Printed in Germany

TITLE:
Darjeeling. View of Jallapahar
PRINTER/PUBLISHER:
Printed in Germany

Bengal, Darjeeling, Sikkim, Assam, Bihar & Orissa

TITLE:
Sikkim. Glacier Head of Langpo Valley

PRINTER/PUBLISHER:
D. Macropolo & Co., Calcutta; printed in Germany

TITLE:
Tista Bridge

36. - Campanile di Badarpur. *Zvonice p.Indi*

TITLE:
*Campanile di Badarpur
(Bell Tower of Badarpur)*

PRINTER/PUBLISHER:
*Società Editrice Internazionale,
Torino (sold for the benefit of the
Salesian Missions)*

MISSIONS SALÉSIENNES

INDES II   7. Préfecture apostolique de l'Assam - Résidence de Gauhati

TITLE:
Prefecture apostolique de l'Assam - Residence de Gauhati (Apostolic Prefecture of Assam - Gauhati Residence)

PRINTER/PUBLISHER:
Salesian Missions, Lyon

POSTAL USAGE:
Within Lyon (France), January 1954

MISSIONI SALESIANE DELL'ASSAM - INDIA - SERIE III.

27. - Gruppo indigeni di Nongba.

TITLE:
Gruppo indigeni di Nongba (Group of Indigenous Nongba)

PRINTER/PUBLISHER:
Societa Editrice Internazionale, Torino (sold for the benefit of the Salesian Missions)

57 Cotton Bales at Tura Market, Assam. (AMERICAN BAPTIST FOREIGN MISSION SOCIETY.)

TITLE:
Cotton Bales at Tura Market, Assam

PRINTER/PUBLISHER:
American Baptist Foreign Mission Society; printed in Japan

Shillong - All Saint Church

TITLE:
Shillong - All Saint Church

PRINTER/PUBLISHER:
Societa Editrice Cartoline, Torino, Italy

Shillong

Government House

Photo by Ghosal Bros., Shillong

TITLE:
Shillong - Government House

PHOTOGRAPHER/ARTIST:
Ghosal Bros, Shillong

MISSIONI SALESIANE DELL'ASSAM - INDIA - SERIE I.

Dům salesiánských missionářů v Indii.

1. - SHILLONG - Prefettura Apostolica.

TITLE:
Shillong - Prefettura Apostolica (Apostolic Prefecture)

PRINTER/PUBLISHER:
Societa Editrice Internazionale, Torino (sold for the benefit of the Salesian Missions)

16. – *Shillong - Loreto Convent*

TITLE:
Shillong - Loreto Convent

PRINTER/PUBLISHER:
Societa Editrice Internazionale,
Torino (sold for the benefit of the
Salesian Missions)

TITLE:
Shillong. The Lake

PRINTER/PUBLISHER:
D. Macropolo & Co., Calcutta; printed in Germany

EXTREME LEFT:

TITLE:
Beadon's Falls, Shillong, Assam

PRINTER/PUBLISHER:
Printed in Austria

LEFT:

TITLE:
Shillong. Lower Elephant Falls

PRINTER/PUBLISHER:
D. Macropolo & Co., Calcutta; printed in Germany

BISHOP'S FALL SHILLONG.

TITLE:
Bishop's Fall Shillong

PRINTER/PUBLISHER:
*Ghoshal Bros, Shillong;
printed in England*

Bengal, Darjeeling, Sikkim, Assam, Bihar & Orissa

Civil Court, Bankipore.

ST. LUKE CHURCH DINAPORE

TITLE:
Budh Gya. Budha under Sacred Tree

PRINTER/PUBLISHER:
D. Macropolo & Co., Calcutta; printed in Germany

Bengal, Darjeeling, Sikkim, Assam, Bihar & Orissa

TITLE:
Gya. View from Phalgu River
PRINTER/PUBLISHER:
D. Macropolo & Co., Calcutta;
printed in Germany

TITLE:
Gaya - Buddha Temple
PRINTER/PUBLISHER:
D.A. Ahuja, Rangoon;
printed in Germany

Streetscene Cuttack, near Waltair   No 434 Publishers Wiele & Klein, Madras

TITLE:
Streetscene Cuttack, near Waltair

PRINTER/PUBLISHER:
Wiele & Klein, Madras;
printed in Saxony

UNDIVIDED BACK

Temple at Bhubaneshwar - 12³⁄₄ hours from Calcutta by the B. N. Rly.

TITLE:
Temple at Bhubaneshwar

PRINTER/PUBLISHER:
The Phototype Co., Bombay

POSTAL USAGE:
Mhow Cantt (India) to Vienna
(Austria), June 1922

Puri, Temple

No. 461   Publishers Wiele & Klein, Madras   Printed in Saxony

TITLE:
Puri, Temple

PRINTER/PUBLISHER:
Wiele & Klein, Madras;
printed in Saxony

UNDIVIDED BACK

Puri. Main Street.

7377. 12 3|4 hours from Calcutta by the B. N. Rly.

TITLE:
Puri. Main Street

POSTAL USAGE:
*Khanag (India) to Lucknow
(India), August 1909*

Surf Boats getting ready to sail out to sea, Seaside Hotel, Puri.

TITLE:
*Surf Boats getting ready to sail out to
sea, Seaside Hotel, Puri*

S. S. "Scindia" Arriving for Cargo, "Flagstaff" Seaside Hotel, Puri.

TITLE:
S.S. "Scindia" Arriving for Cargo,
"Flagstaff" Seaside Hotel, Puri

Das Rasthaus in Koraput.   S. V.

TITLE:
Das Rasthaus in Koraput. S.V.

PRINTER/PUBLISHER:
Printed in Germany

POSTAL USAGE:
Within Germany, June 1914

Im Überschwemmungsgebiet in Indien

Besuch des Missionars in einer armen Dorfschule
in Zentral-Indien

TITLE:
Maiengruss aus Indien - Im überschwemmungsgebiet in Indien/Besuch des missionars in einer armen dorschule in Zentral Indien (Greetings from India - In the flooded area / A missionary visits a poor elementary school in central India)

PRINTER/PUBLISHER:
Missionshaus fur Indien der Missionsbruder des Hl. Franziskus, Haselunne; printed in Saxony

HYDERABAD
MYSORE
&
MADRAS

K. F. Editeurs - Paris

LA POSTE AU DECCAN

The Treaty of Masulipatnam signed in 1768 surrendered the all too important Coromandel coastal region to the East India Company. Hyderabad had become the capital of the nizams in the following year and, by 1798, the Nizam of Hyderabad had signed a subsidiary alliance with the EIC allowing the British India Army to control Bolarum, in modern-day Secunderabad, as a means to protect the state capital of Hyderabad. Secunderabad had developed as a large military cantonment by the early 1900s. About 5 km by road from Secunderabad was Trimulgherry (Tirumalagiri), a strong entrenched camp built to serve as a refuge for all the Europeans of the district in the event of any adverse developments.

The Nizam's State Railway provided the connecting link to the Deccan region from Wadi Junction, a major station on the Bombay to Madras line of the Great Indian Peninsula Railway. With the introduction of the railways in 1880s, several new factories came up in Hyderabad and when, by 1890, even the independent big states of Travancore and Hyderabad came under the control of the EIC, Europeans travelled freely in the entire southern Indian region.

The postcards of Hyderabad capture the powerful Nizam's capital of that time: the palaces and other public buildings, the busy and picturesque street bazaars selling goods made by local artisans around the Char Minar. The Char Minar was originally built to house a college in the upper storeys. The British Residency built

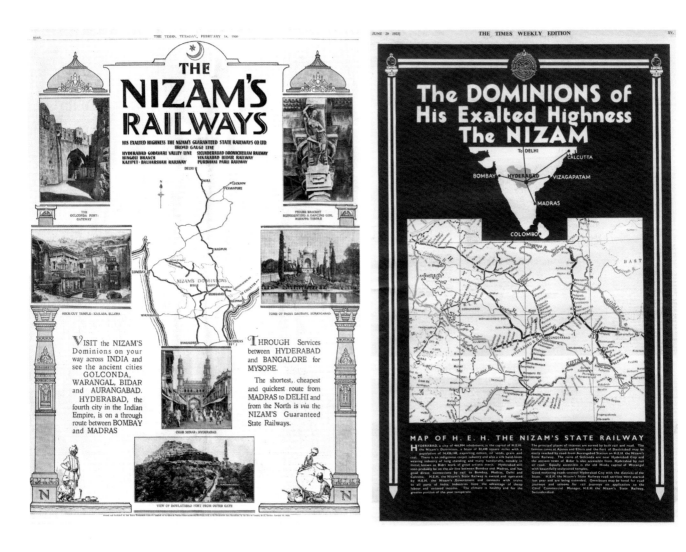

THE NIZAM'S RAILWAYS

HIS EXALTED HIGHNESS THE NIZAM'S GUARANTEED STATE RAILWAYS CO. LTD
BROAD GAUGE LINE

HYDERABAD GODAVARI VALLEY LINE   SECUNDERABAD DRONACHELLAM RAILWAY
HINGOLI BRANCH   VIKARABAD BIDAR RAILWAY
KAZIPET - BALHARSHAH RAILWAY   PURBHANI PARLI RAILWAY

THE GOLCONDA FORT: GATEWAY

FIGURE BRACKET REPRESENTING A DANCING GIRL: RAMAPPA TEMPLE

ROCK-CUT TEMPLE: KAILASA, ELLORA

TOMB OF RABIA DAURANI, AURANGABAD

VISIT the NIZAM'S Dominions on your way across INDIA and see the ancient cities GOLCONDA, WARANGAL, BIDAR and AURANGABAD. HYDERABAD, the fourth city in the Indian Empire, is on a through route between BOMBAY and MADRAS.

THROUGH Services between HYDERABAD and BANGALORE for MYSORE.

The shortest, cheapest and quickest route from MADRAS to DELHI and from the North is *via* the NIZAM'S Guaranteed State Railways.

CHAR MINAR: HYDERABAD

VIEW OF DOWLATABAD FORT FROM OUTER GATE

The DOMINIONS of His Exalted Highness The NIZAM

MAP OF H. E. H. THE NIZAM'S STATE RAILWAY

in 1808 in the suburb of Chander Ghat was located across the Nizam's palace on the banks of the river Musi, which had caused a devastating flood in September 1908, submerging three of the bridges, including the vital Afsal Bridge, featured in a postcard in this series, that had connected the two parts of the city.

The Calcutta to Madras line of the Bengal-Nagpur Railway, constructed through the Eastern Ghats, connected the mineral rich-region of the Raipur Plateau in the Central Provinces to the new sea ports of Vizianagrum, Vizagapatam,

ABOVE:
Advertisement of the Nizam's Railway in The Times, *Weekly Edition (Special India Colour Number), London, 29 June 1933*

ABOVE LEFT:
Advertisement of the Nizam's Railway in the The Times, *Weekly Edition, 18 February 1930*

Bimlapatam and, through a branch line, to Masulipatam. Right through the jute harvest season, Vizianagrum Station operated at maximum capacity, transporting jute on the goods wagons. Early on during the Golden Era of picture postcards, extensive surveys and discussions were underway between the Government of British India, the Government of the Central Provinces and the Railway Board to develop Vizagapatam (Vizag) Port in the backwaters behind the promontory of "Dolphin's Nose", featured in a postcard in this series. Building a land-locked inner harbour at Vizag that would remain well protected from the frequent cyclones that hit the Coromandel Coast seemed highly logical, and eventually the Bengal-Nagpur Railway was sanctioned to build the harbour in 1927. Lord Willingdon, the Governor General and Viceroy of India at that time, inaugurated the harbour on 19 December 1933, and the port went on to provide the sea outlet for the manganese ore of the Central Provinces. Postcards in this series feature Vizagapatam before the construction of the harbour. Waltair, a few kilometers away, was the seaside suburb of Vizagapatam where most of the Europeans resided and where the railway station serving the Vizag Port was located. It became a popular seaside resort for the residents of Madras and was nicknamed "The Brighton of India". The town had all amenities such as clubs and dak bungalows and, like Puri, many seaside bungalows were built with their own rock gardens in the compound.

The railway line from Manmar Junction (on the Bombay to Calcutta line) towards Aurangabad and Secunderabad passed through the town of Deogiri or Daulatabad. A steep road from the 13th-century fortress of Daulatabad had been paved by one of Aurangzeb's courtiers up the hills of Pipal Ghat to Khuldabad, the most important pilgrimage site for the Deccan sultans. This town was earlier known as *Roza / Rauzaa* or "Garden of Paradise" and also as the "Valley of Saints". The postcard of Roza featured in this section shows the tomb of the Sufi saint Zar Zari Zarbaksh who was sent to the Deccan with 700 disciples by Hazrat Nizamuddin Auliya from Delhi, a few years before the first invasion of Deccan by Alauddin Khilji in the 13th century. Over the years, many sufi saints settled here.

Aurangzeb had fortified this once important and prosperous town, abundant with mosques, *nakarkhana*s or music halls, rest houses, schools and tombs of sufi saints, Deccan kings, nobles and generals spread across the town, and chose to be buried here under the open sky near the dargah of his spiritual guide, Sayyad Burhan-ud-din. Hair from the prophet's beard are believed to be preserved in the holy shrine of the sufi saint. As per his wish, Aurangzeb's funeral expenses were met entirely out of the money he had earned by making copies of the Quran and quilting caps anonymously during the last years of his life. When the Viceroy Lord Curzon visited Roza in 1911, he was taken aback by the simplicity of the tomb of the Mughal emperor and ordered the Nizam to encircle the tomb on three sides with a marble railing.

Hotgi Junction, on the Bombay to Madras line, provided connections to the town of Bijapur, well known for its Indo-Saracenic ruins. The town became the district headquarters of the British Raj in 1883. At that time, most of the large and prominent monuments were restored and captured in picture postcards. Some of the smaller palaces and mosques were put to use by the British as a post office or a police station, a dak bungalow or a *cutcherry*.

Early picture postcards of the region cover other sights that, over time, were connected to the railway network: Belgaum (on the Poona to Goa line), Bellary (on the Southern Mahratta Railway line) and the great temple town of Belur/ Balure (on the Hubli to Bangalore line). The prospect of gold mining at Kolar was first brought to the attention of the Mysore British Government in 1850 by a retired Irish soldier, Michael F. Lavelle, from the Bangalore Cantonment, who had served the regiment that had fought against Tipu Sultan at Seringapatam (Srirangapatna). In 1873, he obtained exclusive prospecting rights for mining coal and other metals for 20 years, which he later sold to a syndicate. After a successful stint in gold mining, the affluent and by now extremely popular army man returned home to the Bangalore Cantonment, where the British Commandant named the street where he lived as "Lavelle Road" and his house as "Oorgaum House" after the first shaft that he had sunk to strike gold at Urigaum in the Kolar Gold Fields.

Subsequently, the Kolar district was where railways were first introduced in the state of Mysore. In 1894, the Madras Railway Company built the shortest broad gauge branch line of 16 km called the "Kolar Gold Fields Railway" connecting all the five mining towns between Marikuppam and Bowringpet Junction/Bangarapet, thereby also linking the region to the Bangalore-Madras Railway line. As a result, the movement of mining materials and machinery between the gold fields and the Madras harbour was greatly enhanced. Modern mining techniques had been deployed since 1883 and increased power was harnessed from the Cauvery Falls Power Works.

The Mysore State Railway line from Bangalore to Mysore passed through Seringapatam, the erstwhile capital of the Mysore Kingdom, from the year 1610. With the death of Tipu Sultan in the fourth Anglo-Mysore war in 1799, the capital had shifted to Mysore town. Bangalore functioned as the British capital during the years 1831–81 and developed as the largest military cantonment in southern India, primarily to defend Mysore. The first railway line to connect the state of Mysore to the Madras Presidency, the Bangalore-Madras Railway line, commenced in 1859 from Bangalore Cantonment to Jolarpettai at the initiative of the Chief Commissioner of Mysore State at that time, Colonel Mark Cubbon. The picture postcards of Bangalore capture the polytemporal city—the new English public buildings such as clubs, hotels, hospitals, churches, gardens, and the the growth of the cantonment alongside the existing royal palaces, temples, mosques and markets.

Madras had been an important hub of European presence in southern India, with the French, Portuguese, Danish and Dutch settlements coming up in the early 17th century. In 1639, Francis Day from the EIC purchased the fishing village of Madraspatam for setting up a new trading settlement. As the trading and military presence of the British grew, the base camp of Fort St. George transformed from being Cogan and Day's Castle to being the quadrangular bastioned enclosure of the White Town, to eventually a becoming fortress, which, by 1684, functioned as the seat of the Madras Presidency. Ootacamund functioned as the summer capital of this oldest presidency of India.

Even though Calcutta and Delhi became later-day capitals of British India, it was the Madras Presidency region that they knew best. Bookshops run by Europeans published picture postcards, and hotels and travel/tour companies in the region popularised them amongst the European residents and visitors. It is from this city that the "Indo-Saracenic" style of architecture began in India with the construction of the Chepauk Palace in the 1760s, featured in this series in a pre-1907 postcard. Many postcards carried images of these "European versions of Oriental Palaces" built in Madras as prominent government buildings. Postcards of Madras also captured the traditional culture: temples bustling with devotees, festivals at Mylapore and Triplicane, the busy harbour and markets, and people filling up the long promenade of Marina Beach. Photographers captured the picturesque with the palm-studded Cooum River banks and the coastline dotted with the characteristic masula boats and catamarans that are still used for fishing all along the Coromandel Coast. The European artists and photographers were quite fascinated with the skill of the fishermen in navigating the surf on these precarious-looking boats that were made quite simply by tying together wooden planks with coir.

Trips from Madras to Mahabalipuram or the Seven Pagodas were popular by boat through the Buckingham Canal, an important waterway during the late 1800s and early 1900s. The canal ran parallel to the Coromandel Coast, connecting most of the natural backwaters to the port.

The first section of the railway journey from Madras to the Nilgiris or "Blue Mountains", the point of convergence of the Eastern and Western Ghats, was facilitated by the Nilgiri branch of the Madras Railway. The train passed through Coimbatore, thereafter crossed the 32-km wide gap in the ghats at Palghat, an important trading town of Malabar, and then terminated at Mettupalayam.

From Mettupalayam, the metre gauge Nilgiri Mountain Railway, which was inaugurated in 1908, took travellers up to the hills through a 7,300-foot ascent over 46 km in about four to five hours at that time, with its engine attached at the rear.

The celebrated railway journey, which is now part of the Mountain Railways of India UNESCO World Heritage Site, passed through numerous bends, tunnels, bridges and waterfalls and was well captured in early picture postcards.

The first station of Coonoor, situated on the lower ridge, was popular for its mild climate with Indians as well at that time. Picnic parties were held at Sim's Park, Dolphin's Nose, Kateri Falls, Lady Canning Seat, etc. The mountain railway continued to the military cantonment of Wellington and terminated at Ootacamund, the summer capital of the presidency, at an altitude of 7,500 feet. The name is believed to be derived from its earlier names of *Whotakaymund/ Wootacamund/Wuttasamund/Ottakalmandu,* as it was referred to at the time when the hills were inhabited by the aboriginal Todas. The language and customs of the Todas remained a subject of extensive ethnographical and historical study by the Europeans during the British Raj.

Ootacamund or Ooty (as later shortened by the British), the "Queen of Hill Stations" with its well-laid-out gardens, was well equipped with all civic amenities and filled with activities and entertainment in the summer months, such as evening dances, cinemas, tennis, golf, races, the celebrated flower shows, the hotly contested dog shows, hunting and fishing. In fact, one governor of Madras in the 1850s had unsuccessfully tried to rechristen Ooty as "Victoria"! Most of the expansion of the town happened in the 1860s, as individuals and later the British Government steadily acquired land from the Todas (on an average for about one rupee per acre), transforming the hills into a military sanitarium. The famous Orientalist, writer, poet, explorer, ethnologist and diplomat Richard Francis Burton was also sent up to Ooty on sick leave in 1847, while he was serving as a lieutenant in the British Army. The uphill journey to Ooty by road from Coimbatore or Mysore was popular too, with travellers stopping along the way at dak bungalows for rest and refreshments.

Picnics to Pykara Falls, about 28 km from Ooty, through a good motor road were popular. The power generated from the hydroelectric works at the falls was supplied to many districts in South India.

The South Indian Railway from Madras to Tuticorin (Thoothukudi) passed through French Pondicherry and Danish Tranquebar. There are numerous pre-1907 undivided back postcards of French Pondicherry published on behalf of the Maritime Messaging Service. French mail steamers called regularly at Pondicherry at that time.

Remnants of old Danish occupation could still be seen at Tranquebar, but the port was losing out in importance to Negapatam at the time of the Golden Era of picture postcards. The first Protestant mission in India was founded at Tranquebar

Advertisement issued by the South Indian Railway in The Times, India Number, *London, 18 February 1930*

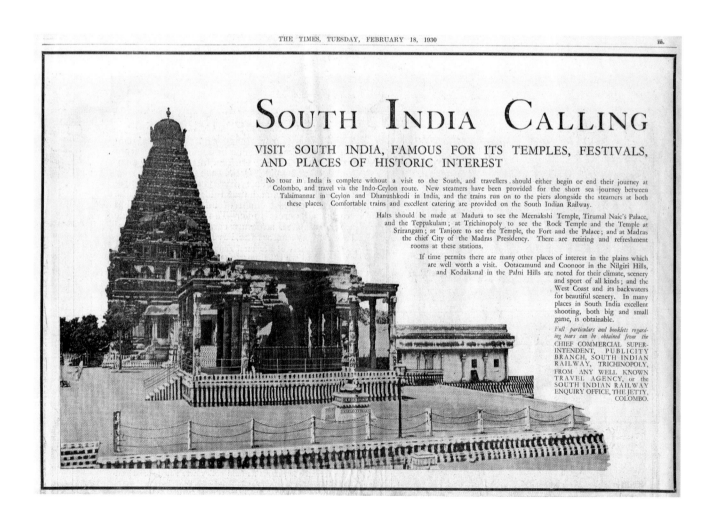

THE TIMES, TUESDAY, FEBRUARY 18, 1930   iii.

SOUTH INDIA CALLING

VISIT SOUTH INDIA, FAMOUS FOR ITS TEMPLES, FESTIVALS, AND PLACES OF HISTORIC INTEREST

No tour in India is complete without a visit to the South, and travellers should either begin or end their journey at Colombo, and travel via the Indo-Ceylon route. New steamers have been provided for the short sea journey between Talaimannar in Ceylon and Dhanushkodi in India, and the trains run on to the piers alongside the steamers at both these places. Comfortable trains and excellent catering are provided on the South Indian Railway.

Halts should be made at Madura to see the Meenakshi Temple, Tirumal Naic's Palace, and the Teppakulam; at Trichinopoly to see the Rock Temple and the Temple at Srirangam; at Tanjore to see the Temple, the Fort and the Palace; and at Madras the chief City of the Madras Presidency. There are retiring and refreshment rooms at these stations.

If time permits there are many other places of interest in the plains which are well worth a visit. Ootacamund and Coonoor in the Nilgiri Hills, and Kodaikanal in the Palni Hills are noted for their climate, scenery and sport of all kinds; and the West Coast and its backwaters for beautiful scenery. In many places in South India excellent shooting, both big and small game, is obtainable.

Full particulars and booklets regarding tours can be obtained from the CHIEF COMMERCIAL SUPERINTENDENT, PUBLICITY BRANCH, SOUTH INDIAN RAILWAY, TRICHINOPOLY, FROM ANY WELL KNOWN TRAVEL AGENCY, or the SOUTH INDIAN RAILWAY ENQUIRY OFFICE, THE JETTY, COLOMBO.

in 1706 and, interestingly, the postcard of Tranquebar featured in this series was published by the Evangelic Lutheran mission at Leipzig, Germany, as part of church propaganda.

The South Indian Railway line continued to the beautiful temple towns of Chidambaram, Mayaveram, Kumbakonam, Tanjore, Trichinopoly, the island town of Srirangam that lay along the bifurcation of the river Cauvery, and onwards to Madura (Madurai). Photographers captured the picturesque–the views of these sacred cities that lay amidst lush palm trees and paddy fields, dotted with colourful and richly carved temple *gopurams*, with their characteristic pillared *mandapams*, holy tanks and the rituals that formed an integral part of the lives of the people. Several postcards capture the religious iconography of the temples in detail. The study of the religious texts of India and their translation had already become an integral part of Oriental studies pursued by Europeans by the time of the Golden Era of picture postcards. Trips to Kodaikanal at a height of 7,000 feet in the Palni Hills were made from Madurai through Ammayanayakanur.

Railway Station Hyderabad, Dn.

TITLE:
Railway Station Hyderabad, Dn.

PRINTER/PUBLISHER:
Printed in Saxony

Char Minde Hyderabad (Deccan)

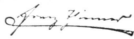

Souvenir of East Indies 73

TITLE:
Souvenir of East Indies - Char Minde Hyderabad (Deccan)

UNDIVIDED BACK

POSTAL USAGE:
Hyderabad (India) to Innsbruck (Austria), November 1895

STREET AT HYDERABAD.

TITLE:
Street at Hyderabad
PRINTER/PUBLISHER:
Printed in Germany
UNDIVIDED BACK

Pathergatti, Hyderabad, Dn.

TITLE:
Pathergatti, Hyderabad, Dn.
PRINTER/PUBLISHER:
*Picture Stall, Hyderabad Dn.;
printed in Germany*

Basherbagh Palace. Hyderabad, Dn.

The Residency. Hyderabad, Dn.

Hyderabad, Mysore & Madras

313

H. H. THE NIZAM LEAVING THE RESIDENCY, HYDERABAD.

TITLE:
H.H. The Nizam Leaving the Residency, Hyderabad
PRINTER/PUBLISHER:
printed in Saxony

Leibgarde Sr. Hoheit des Nizam vonHyderabad (Deccan)

Souvenir of East Indies 74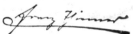

TITLE:
Souvenir of East Indies - Leibgarde Sr. Hoheit des Nizam vonHyderabad Deccan (Bodyguards of his Highness the Nizam of Hyderabad Deccan)
UNDIVIDED BACK
POSTAL USAGE:
Hyderabad (India) to Dresden (Germany), September 1901

Afserjungs Bungalow A Hyderabad (Deccan)

TITLE:
Afserjungs Bungalow
A Hyderabad (Deccan)

PRINTER/PUBLISHER:
The Phototype Co., Bombay;
printed in Luxembourg

River View from Afzalgunj Bridge. Hyderabad Dn.

TITLE:
River View from Afzalgunj Bridge.
Hyderabad Dn.

PRINTER/PUBLISHER:
Printed in Saxony

TOMBS AT GOLCONDA, HYDERABAD.

TITLE:
Tombs at Golconda, Hyderabad

PRINTER/PUBLISHER:
Printed in Germany

UNDIVIDED BACK

Railway Station. Secunderabad

TITLE:
Railway Station. Secunderabad

PRINTER/PUBLISHER:
Printed in Saxony

JAMES BAZAAR STREET, SECUNDERABAD.

TITLE:
James Bazaar Street, Secunderabad

PRINTER/PUBLISHER:
Printed in Germany

UNDIVIDED BACK

OVERFLOW HASSAIN SAGUR TANK, SECUNDERABAD.

TITLE:
*Overflow Hassain Sagur Tank,
Secunderabad*

PRINTER/PUBLISHER:
Printed in Germany

UNDIVIDED BACK

ONE TREE HILL, SECUNDERABAD.

TITLE:
One Tree Hill, Secunderabad

PRINTER/PUBLISHER:
Printed in Germany

UNDIVIDED BACK

St. Patricks R. C. Chapel, Trimulgherry

TITLE:
St. Patricks R.C. Chapel,
Trimulgherry

PRINTER/PUBLISHER:
Printed in Saxony

Post Office. Trimulgherry

CHANDULAL'S CAR, BOLARUM, HYDERABAD.

BAZAAR AND CLOCK TOWER. VIZIANAGARAM.　　M. RATHNAM & CO., VIZAG.

The Town from Ross' Hill, Vizagapatam

7242　22 Hours from Calcutta by the B. N. Rly.

TITLE:
Bazaar and Clock Tower -
Vizianagaram
PRINTER/PUBLISHER:
M. Rathnam & Co., Vizag

TITLE:
The Town from Ross'
Hill, Vizagapatam

The Beach, Vizagapatam

Exchange a few black rocks and a fort jutting out into the sea, for the lighthouse & hills in the background & this might be Colombo of our memory. Shall send more from Calcutta by the B. N. Rly.

TITLE:
The Beach, Vizagapatam

POSTAL USAGE:
To London (UK)

QUEEN'S STATUE VIZAG.

M. RATHNAM AND CO. VIZAG.

TITLE:
Queen's Statue Vizag

PRINTER/PUBLISHER:
M. Rathnam & Co., Vizag

TITLE:
*Scandal Point &
Daulphins Nose, Vizag*

PRINTER/PUBLISHER:
M. Rathnam & Co., Vizag

TITLE:
*A general view Fort Doulatabad,
Hyderabad Deccan (India)*

PRINTER/PUBLISHER:
*H. A. Mirza & Sons, Delhi;
printed in Germany*

TITLE:
Tomb of Zurdani Zurbuksh, Rosa

PRINTER/PUBLISHER:
Combridge & Co., Bombay

UNDIVIDED BACK

166. Tomb of Zurdani Zurbuksh, Rosa Combridge & Co., Bombay

TITLE:
Jumma Musjid, Bijapur

PRINTER/PUBLISHER:
Clifton & Co., Bombay

UNDIVIDED BACK

JUMMA MUSJID, BIJAPUR. Clifton & Co.

MALIK-I-MAIDAN, BIJAPUR.

Clifton & Co.

TITLE:
Malik-i-Maidan, Bijapur
PRINTER/PUBLISHER:
Clifton & Co., Bombay
UNDIVIDED BACK

The Fort, Belgaum

TITLE:
The Fort, Belgaum
PRINTER/PUBLISHER:
Printed in Saxony

45. THE S. RAMPART & MOAT, BELGAUM

TITLE:
The S. Rampart & Moat, Belgaum

PRINTER/PUBLISHER:
S. Mahadeo & Son, Belgaum;
printed in Saxony

The Fort Church, Belgaum.

TITLE:
The Fort Church, Belgaum

PRINTER/PUBLISHER:
Printed in Saxony

TITLE:
British Infantry Lines Bellary

PRINTER/PUBLISHER:
Printed in Saxony

Balure, Temple

No. 470   Publishers Wiele & Klein, Madras

Printed in Saxony

TITLE:
Balure Temple

PRINTER/PUBLISHER:
*Wiele & Klein, Madras;
printed in Saxony*

UNDIVIDED BACK

Muhammadanische Moschee in Kolar.

TITLE:
Muhammadanische Moschee in Kolar
(Mohammedan Mosque in Kolar)

PRINTER/PUBLISHER:
Catholic Mission Friends
for India, Vienna

Del Tufo & Co., S. India.

Sally Port where Tippoo fell Seringapatam.

TITLE:
Sally Port where Tippoo fell
Seringapatam

PRINTER/PUBLISHER:
Del Tufo & Co., South India

UNDIVIDED BACK

Moslem erected over the remains of Tippoo Seringapatam.

TITLE:
Moslem erected over the remains of Tippoo Seringapatam

PRINTER/PUBLISHER:
Del Tufo & Co., South India

UNDIVIDED BACK

Raja Tipoo's Observatory, Bangalore

TITLE:
Raja Tipoo's Observatory, Bangalore

PRINTER/PUBLISHER:
Printed in Saxony

TITLE:
Lit up Mysore Palace

POSTAL USAGE:
*Vepery (India) to Czech Republic,
April 1959*

Cubbon Park I have been round to all these places. Very pretty.
I am to be married on 6th Sep: so please note my new address on other card
Helm? P n

Wiele's Studio, Bangalore

TITLE:
Cubbon Park

PRINTER/PUBLISHER:
Printed in Germany

PHOTOGRAPHER/ARTIST:
Wiele's Studio, Bangalore

POSTAL USAGE:
*Within Bangalore (India),
August 1915*

ROYAL PALACE, BANGALORE.

The Maharani's Hospital

Wiele's Studio, Bangalore

TITLE:
The Maharani's Hospital

PRINTER/PUBLISHER:
Printed in Germany

PHOTOGRAPHER/ARTIST:
Wiele's Studio, Bangalore

BANGALORE.
COMMERCIAL STREET.

TITLE:
Bangalore. Commercial Street

PRINTER/PUBLISHER:
Raphael Tuck & Sons, London; printed in England

POSTAL USAGE:
Bombay (India) to USA, July 1951

TITLE:
Commercial Street, Bangalore
PRINTER/PUBLISHER:
Printed in Saxony

TITLE:
British Soldier's Club, Bangalore
PRINTER/PUBLISHER:
Printed in Saxony

The Race Stand, Bangalore

West End Hotel. Bangalore.

The Picture House, 3 Brigade Road. Bangalore.

TITLE:
West End Hotel, Bangalore

PHOTOGRAPHER/ARTIST:
The Picture House, Bangalore

POSTAL USAGE:
Bombay (India) to Boston (USA), May 1913

10 b. The Blighty Tea Rooms, Bangalore.   S. Mahadeo & Son, Belgaum

TITLE:
The Blighty Tea Rooms, Bangalore

PRINTER/PUBLISHER:
Printed in Germany

PHOTOGRAPHER/ARTIST:
S. Mahadeo & Son, Belgaum

Post Office, Bangalore.

TITLE:
Post Office, Bangalore

PRINTER/PUBLISHER:
T. Mamundy Pillay & Sons, Bangalore; processed in Prussia

St. Mark's Church, Bangalore.

TITLE:
St. Marks Church, Bangalore

PRINTER/PUBLISHER:
English Emporium, Bangalore; printed in England by Raphael Tuck & Sons, London

TITLE:
Trinity Church

PRINTER/PUBLISHER:
Printed in Germany

PHOTOGRAPHER/ARTIST:
Wiele's Studio, Bangalore

TITLE:
Bangalore. Somesware Temple, Alsur

PRINTER/PUBLISHER:
*Raphael Tuck & Sons, London;
printed in England*

Muthia Lamma Goddess, Bangalore

TITLE:
Muthia Lamma Goddess, Bangalore

POSTAL USAGE:
Meerut (India) to Prague (Czech Republic), March 1910

TITLE:
Lubbay Musjid, Bangalore

PRINTER/PUBLISHER:
Printed in Saxony

TITLE:
Bird's Eye View of Madras from the Light-house

PRINTER/PUBLISHER:
Wiele & Klein, Madras; printed in Germany

MADRAS.
MYLAPORE TANK.

TITLE:
Madras. Mylapore Tank

PRINTER/PUBLISHER:
*Raphael Tuck & Sons, London;
printed in England*

Main Gopuram, Madras.

TITLE:
Main Gopuram, Madras

Holy Car Procession.   Triplicane.
Madras.

TITLE:
*Holy Car Procession.
Triplicane. Madras*

PRINTER/PUBLISHER:
*Wiele & Klein, Madras;
printed in Germany*

Zoroastrian Temple

TITLE:
Zoroastrian Temple

PRINTER/PUBLISHER:
*The Theosophical Society,
Adyar, Madras*

POSTAL USAGE:
India to Czech Republic, 1930s

MOWBRAY'S ROAD, MADRAS.

92290

DATE PALMS, MADRAS.

W. AND K., MADRAS.   No. 43.—Date Palms, Chepauk.

TITLE:
Date Palms, Chepauk
PRINTER/PUBLISHER:
Wiele & Klein, Madras
UNDIVIDED BACK

THE CHEPAUK PALACE, MADRAS.

92299

TITLE:
The Chepauk Palace, Madras
UNDIVIDED BACK

The Presidency College, Madras.   Higginbotham & Co., Madras & Bangalore.   No. 222.

TITLE:
The Presidency College, Madras

PRINTER/PUBLISHER:
*Higginbotham & Co.,
Madras and Bangalore*

POSTAL USAGE:
*Madras (India) to Roulers
(Belgium), October 1907*

Government House, Madras.

TITLE:
Government House, Madras

PRINTER/PUBLISHER:
Printed abroad

Y. M. C. A., Madras. No. 9. Carnatic Studio, P. S. Sastri & Co., Madras.

TITLE:
Y.M.C.A., Madras

PRINTER/PUBLISHER:
Carnatic Studio, P.S. Sastri & Co., Madras; printed in Saxony

Bank of Madras.

TITLE:
Bank of Madras

PRINTER/PUBLISHER:
Printed abroad

Moore Market, Madras.

93168 Higginbotham & Co., Madras & Bangalore. No. 4.

TITLE:
Moore Market, Madras

PRINTER/PUBLISHER:
*Higginbotham & Co.,
Madras and Bangalore*

Esplanade. Madras.

TITLE:
Esplanade, Madras

PRINTER/PUBLISHER:
Printed abroad

Ladies Boat Club, Madras.

TITLE:
Ladies Boat Club, Madras

PRINTER/PUBLISHER:
*Whiteaway Laidlaw & Co. Ltd,
Madras; processed in Saxony by
Raphael Tuck & Sons, London*

Der Fluß Cooum mit dem Senathause in Madras.

TITLE:
*Der Fluss Cooum mit dem Senathause
in Madras (The River Cooum with
the Senate House in Madras)*

PRINTER/PUBLISHER:
*Catholic Mission
Friends for India, Vienna*

POSTAL USAGE:
*Auersthal (Austria) to Tyrol
(Austria), August 1918*

First Line Beach, Madras.

97557 Higginbotham & Co., Madras & Bangalore No. 109.

TITLE:
First Line Beach, Madras
PRINTER/PUBLISHER:
Higginbotham & Co.,
Madras and Bangalore

FIRST LINE BEACH, MADRAS.

Clifton & Co.

TITLE:
First Line Beach, Madras
PRINTER/PUBLISHER:
Clifton & Co., Bombay
UNDIVIDED BACK

VIEW FROM LANDING PLACE, MADRAS.

TITLE:
View from Landing Place, Madras

UNDIVIDED BACK

92307

Early morning, Madras Beach

No. 45   Publishers Wiele & Klein, Madras   Printed in Saxony

TITLE:
Early morning, Madras Beach

PRINTER/PUBLISHER:
Wiele & Klein, Madras; printed in Saxony

UNDIVIDED BACK

MASULA BOAT, MADRAS.

TITLE:
Masula Boat, Madras

UNDIVIDED BACK

Del Tufo & Co., S. India.

Catamaran, Madras.

TITLE:
Catamaran, Madras

PRINTER/PUBLISHER:
Del Tufo & Co., S. India

UNDIVIDED BACK

Hotel d'Angelis - Madras

TITLE:
Hotel d'Angelis - Madras

PRINTER/PUBLISHER:
Trau & Schwab, Dresden;
printed in Saxony

The Connemara Hotel, Madras   No. 48   Publishers Wiele & Klein, Madras

Printed in Saxony

TITLE:
The Connemara Hotel, Madras

PRINTER/PUBLISHER:
Wiele & Klein, Madras;
printed in Saxony

UNDIVIDED BACK

TITLE:
Connemara

POSTAL USAGE:
India to Prague (Czech Republic), 1950s

Temples at Seven Pagodas.   Higginbotham & Co., Madras & Bangalore. No. 321.

TITLE:
Temples at Seven Pagodas

PRINTER/PUBLISHER:
Higginbotham & Co., Madras and Bangalore

A TEMPLE, SEVEN PAGODAS.

TITLE:
Temple on the Sea Shore - A temple, Seven Pagodas

UNDIVIDED BACK

POSTAL USAGE:
Bombay (India) to Naples (Italy), December 1903

Street Scene, Palghat

No. 501   Publishers Wiele & Klein, Madras

TITLE:
Street Scene, Palghat

PRINTER/PUBLISHER:
Wiele & Klein, Madras; printed in Saxony

UNDIVIDED BACK

Kartari Tunnel Nilgiri Railway

Nilgiri Railway, Half Tunnel

TITLE:
Kartari Tunnel Nilgiri Railway

PRINTER/PUBLISHER:
H.W. West, Coonoor;
printed in Germany

TITLE:
Nilgiri Railway, Half Tunnel

PRINTER/PUBLISHER:
H.W. West, Coonoor;
printed in Germany

Nilgiri Railway Bridge

Lambs Rock

TITLE:
Nilgiri Railway Bridge

PRINTER/PUBLISHER:
H.W. West, Coonoor;
printed in Germany

TITLE:
Lambs Rock

PRINTER/PUBLISHER:
H.W. West, Coonoor;
printed in Germany

Wenlock Bridge

The Pykara Falls, Nilgiris.
Higginbotham & Co., Madras & Bangalore. No. 190A.

TITLE:
Wenlock Bridge

PRINTER/PUBLISHER:
H.W. West, Coonoor;
printed in Germany

TITLE:
The Pykara Falls, Nilgiris

PRINTER/PUBLISHER:
Higginbotham & Co.,
Madras and Bangalore

Benhope Falls

TITLE:
Benhope Falls

PRINTER/PUBLISHER:
H.W. West, Coonoor;
printed in Germany

Approach to Coonoor.

TITLE:
Approach to Coonoor

POSTAL USAGE:
Saharanpur (India) to Zurich
(Switzerland), December 1930

Coonoor.

Coonoor East View Shundy Bazaar

Sims Park Lake, Early Morning, Coonoor.

Hyderabad, Mysore & Madras

Ootacamund—General View.

Higginbotham & Co. Madras & Bangalore. No. 191.

TITLE:
Ootacamund - General View

PRINTER/PUBLISHER:
*Higginbotham & Co.,
Madras and Bangalore*

PANORAMIC VIEW, OOTACAMUND.

TITLE:
Panoramic View, Ootacamund

PRINTER/PUBLISHER:
*D.B. Taraporevala and Sons,
Bombay; printed in Saxony*

UNDIVIDED BACK

POSTAL USAGE:
*Bombay (India) to Tehran (Iran),
September 1907*

RACE COURSE GYMKHANA, OOTACAMUND

TITLE:
Race Course Gymkhana, Ootacamund

UNDIVIDED BACK

Government House Gardens, Ootacamund

Higginbotham & Co., Madras & Bangalore.

TITLE:
Government House Gardens, Ootacamund

PRINTER/PUBLISHER:
Higginbotham & Co., Madras and Bangalore

POSTAL USAGE:
Dehradun (India) to Prague (Czech Republic), July 1921

St. Thomas Church, Ootacamund

TITLE:
St. Thomas Church, Ootacamund

PRINTER/PUBLISHER:
Dinshaw H. Hazary, Ootacamund; printed in Germany

Group of Todas, Ootacamund.

Higginbotham & Co., Madras & Bangalore. No. 21.

TITLE:
Group of Todas, Ootacamund

PRINTER/PUBLISHER:
Higginbotham & Co., Madras and Bangalore

L'Inde des Rajas

Dans les Vindhya. - MARIAPOUR, le village des orphelins de la famine

TITLE:
L'Inde des Rajas; Dans les Vindhya - Mariapour, le village des orphelins de la famine (India of the Rajas; In Vindhya - Mariapour, the village of orphans from famine)

Photo ateliers, Baudouin Vincent Marseille

47 Pondichery - *Le Clocher du Grand Bazar*

TITLE:
Pondichery - Le Clocher du Grand Bazar (The Belltower of Grand Bazaar)

PHOTOGRAPHER/ARTIST:
Baudouin Vincent Marseille

UNDIVIDED BACK

21.- Pondichéry - Place du Gouvernement, Fontaine et Hôtel

53 Pondichery - *L'Etang de la Pagode de Villenour*

TITLE:
Les plus anciennes colonies françaises: Pagode de Vilnour a Pondichery (The oldest French colonies: Temple of Vilnour in Pondichery)

PRINTER/PUBLISHER:
Chicorée nouvelle et moka casiez, hors-concours, Casiez - Bourgeois, Cambrai (Nord); Imp. H. Laas, E. Pecaud & Co., Paris

UNDIVIDED BACK

TITLE:
Divinites indiennes de Canicovil, pres Pondichery (Indian deities of Canicovil, near Pondicherry)

UNDIVIDED BACK

6 Pondichery -   *Revue de l'Artillerie des Cipahis*
                    sur la Place du Gouvernement

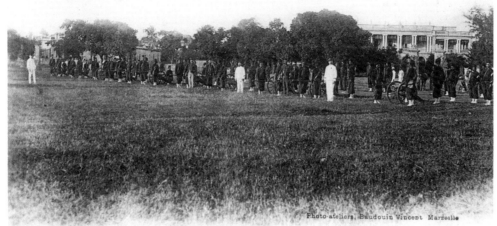

Photo-ateliers, Baudouin Vincent Marzeille

TITLE:
Pondichery - Revue de l'Artillerie des Cipahis sur la place du Gouvernement (Review of Artillery of Cipahis at the Government Square)

PHOTOGRAPHER/ARTIST:
Baudouin Vincent Marseille

UNDIVIDED BACK

POSTAL USAGE:
Pondicherry (India) to Calcutta (India), March 1909

TITLE:
Konigstrasse in Trankebar, Ostindien (King's Street in Tranquebar, East India)

PRINTER/PUBLISHER:
Evangelic Lutheran Mission, Leipzig; printed in Saxony

Srirungam Temples.

Higginbotham & Co., Madras & Bangalore. No. 157.

TITLE:
Srirungam Temples

PRINTER/PUBLISHER:
*Higginbotham & Co.,
Madras and Bangalore*

The Rayagopuram, Srirungum.

Higginbotham & Co., Madras & Bangalore. No. 3034.

TITLE:
The Rayagopuram, Srirungum

PRINTER/PUBLISHER:
*Higginbotham & Co.,
Madras and Bangalore*

KODAIKANAL.

Aunt Margaret –
With love from Horace & Flor

TITLE:
Kodaikanal
UNDIVIDED BACK

Eagle Cliff, Kodaikanal.   Higginbotham & Co., Madras & Bangalore.   No. 291

TITLE:
Eagle Cliff, Kodaikanal
PRINTER/PUBLISHER:
*Higginbotham & Co.,
Madras and Bangalore*

Menachi Temple. Madura.

MADURA. PRINCIPAL GOPURAM AND COURT. MD 1678.

TITLE:
Menachi Temple, Madura

PRINTER/PUBLISHER:
Printed abroad

TITLE:
Madura. Principal Gopuram and Court

PRINTER/PUBLISHER:
D. Macropolo & Co., Calcutta; printed in Germany

POSTAL USAGE:
India to Prague (Czech Republic), January 1912

Golden
Lily Tank
Madura.

TITLE:
Golden Lily Tank, Madura

PRINTER/PUBLISHER:
Higginbotham & Co.,
Madras and Bangalore

POSTAL USAGE:
Triplicane (India) to Prague (Czech
Republic), December 1906

A Temple Garudasthumbum (Flagstaff).
Higginbotham & Co., Madras & Bangalore. No. 332.

TITLE:
A Temple Garudasthumbum
(Flagstaff)

PRINTER/PUBLISHER:
Higginbotham & Co.,
Madras and Bangalore

St-Mary's Mother of dolours' church. - MADURA

Hyderabad, Mysore & Madras

PICTURE POSTCARD PHOTOGRAPHERS, PRINTERS AND PUBLISHERS

"If card-players will not be enlightened, why should card-makers fret themselves there at? Messrs. De la Rue are said to have spent much capital, and much time and ingenuity, in producing more graceful figures than those now seen on our court-cards; they have employed talented artists, and have produced many novelties; but people will not give up the old deformities, and therefore deformities are still made to please the people."

—*A Pack of Cards*, Charles Dickens

From playing cards to postcards, stamps and government stationery, and finally on to being the world's largest commercial banknotes and passports manufacturer, the transition of the English company *De La Rue* is a fascinating journey in the history of commercial printing outside the world of books and newspapers printing.

Thomas De la Rue was a French printer who moved to England in 1821, where, initially, he tried his hand at newspaper and book printing. In 1828, he set up a playing cards production company and introduced new techniques like letter-press printing and water-marking. Over time, they became the biggest playing card manufacturers in the Empire.

Around 1840, English printer *Perkins, Bacon & Co.* was the sole producer of the first English stamps—Penny Black and Red. By 1855, however, the East India Company had instead signed up Messrs. De La Rue & Company to manufacture and supply stamps for India. By 1879, they expanded the scope to include all embossed envelopes, postcards (British India postcards only) and other government stationery.

The company opened an office in Calcutta, where production was also undertaken. The contracts of De La Rue & Company were renewed all the way until 1925, when the Nashik press for printing Indian postal stationery, stamps and banknotes was set up.

British India postcards that came into use from 1879 were solely produced by De La Rue & Company. These were of two denominations—the "quarter-anna card" for domestic use and the "one and a half-anna card" for countries affiliated to the Universal Postal Union, which had come into existence in June 1878.

The first set of postcards produced by De la Rue were on straw-card, to avoid forgery. The quarter-anna card had the inscription "East India Post Card" with the British coat-of-arms in the center and a stamp with the diamond crown of Queen Victoria on the upper right corner, printed in red-brown. The international postcards had a title "Universal Postal Union" in English and French at the top centre, and the bilingual inscriptions of "British India Postcard" below the top line were separated by the coat-of-arms, with the stamp placed in the right hand corner, all printed in blue. In 1899, as picture postcards issued by private publishers came into circulation, the word "East" was removed and the title became "India Post Card".

The challenges faced by the British amidst the diversity of India in introducing a single currency and coinage, and mitigating the risk of forgery also led them to necessitate the centralisation of production of all British India postal stationery to the De La Rue & Company in 1855. One of the most famous errors in the postal history of this region had taken place in Mauritius with the famous "penny stamp". It all began with the Governor of Mauritius and his wife, Lady Gomm, planning a ball at the Government House on 30 September 1847. Lady Gomm had noticed the new invention—the penny stamps that were pasted on envelopes which she had been receiving from England—and thought would it be a novel idea to send her invitations with similar stamps, but marked "Mauritius". The local watchmaker and lithographer Joseph Barnard was tasked to engrave orange-red one-penny and deep-blue two-penny stamps. With a single plate, each stamp was individually engraved, but in the rush, Barnard engraved "Post Office" instead of "Post Paid" on the stamps. Nobody noticed this error until it was too late and the invitations with these erroneous stamps were sent out to addresses in Bombay and other parts of British India. Today, these Mauritius stamps are one of the most coveted items for collectors across the world. One such invitation letter with the erroneous two-penny stamp that had been sent to an address in Bombay came up for an auction at New York in October 1968. Five famous philatelists—Raymond H. Weill of New Orleans, Stanley Gibbons of London, Renato Mondolfo of Italy, Robert Siegel of New York, and Giulio Bolaffi of Italy participated in the bidding, expecting it to close at \$20,000, but in the end Raymond Weill won it for \$3,80,000.

While the production of the postcard and postage stamps continued to be centralised with India Post, since the days of its transition from De La Rue Company to the Nasik production center in 1925, the production of picture postcards had been decentralised right from inception. With image printing expertise already available in Central Europe, private British postcard manufacturers often outsourced the postcard production to German firms, especially in the Saxony area, or to Austria. Other early Indian picture postcard sellers did the same. In fact, many of them already had production tie-ups with European firms for producing God pictures and trade labels.

As photography costs reduced and printing technology and skills came into India, numerous picture postcard companies were set up in India to capture the Indian topography, ethnography and architecture. Photographers, book publishers and booksellers took the lead, and they usually specialised in their respective geographies, i.e. their own cities and the areas around them.

German, Dutch, Danish, Portuguese, Italian, French and English Christian missionaries had been present in India from early times and these institutions published their own postcards that captured in images the work they were doing in India.

Discussed below is a brief description of the pioneers in Indian picture postcard printing and publishing, listed in alphabetical order.

B.K. Abdul & Co., Ranikhet
Publisher

Published postcards of the town of Ranikhet and the landscapes around. Their postcards were printed in Saxony.

D.A. Ahuja, Rangoon (1885–early 20th century)
Commercial Photographer

D.A. Ahuja was the most prominent Indian photographer to work in Burma. The firm, established in 1885 as Kundan Dass & Co., changed its name to D.A. Ahuja in 1900. The studio was located at Maha Bandoola Road, Rangoon. To the studio's credit are over 800 images of Burmese landscapes, temples and individual portraits of the Burmese people. His photographs and postcards were mailed out to locations throughout the British Empire, providing the English-speaking world with snapshots of the varied Burmese tribes and their dressing styles.

Ahuja took great care to have the best German printers turn his photographs into deeply coloured and textured images. This set him a class apart from the early Asian image publishers. Besides publishing photographs of his own, Ahuja published earlier photographs taken by Klier, and Watts & Skeen. Ahuja also became the proprietor of the firm Watts & Skeen in 1912.

In the later years, several cheap duplications of Ahuja's elegant compositions started appearing to cater to the tourist markets. Today, about 200 original images produced by Ahuja are part of the archives of the Pitt Rivers Museum, University of Oxford.

Art Union, Calcutta
Publisher

Art Union, situated in Sir Stuart Hogg Market, published fine topographical postcards of Calcutta. They showcased the city's people and professions, capturing its unique culture during the 1920s.

Baljee
Photographer and Publisher

Baljee was a fine photographer and postcard publisher with studios in Rawalpindi and Murree. The studio published a large number of postcards of northern India and Gujarat. Some of their postcards were hand-tinted.

G. C. Banerjee & Sons, Kurseong
Publisher

Publisher of postcards of Kurseong and the Darjeeling area in the early 1900s. Their postcards were printed in Germany.

Thos. H. Bell
Commercial Photographer

Thos. H. Bell extensively photographed Chakrata, and was the commercial photographer employed by publishers Moorli Dhar & Sons.

Bourne & Shepherd, Calcutta, Simla and Bombay (1863–20th century)
Commercial Photographer

Bourne & Shepherd was one of the oldest, most successful and influential commercial photography studios in India in the 19th century. Exhibiting a high level of finesse in photography and its printing, the studio was appointed as official photographers of the British Government, Indian royalty and noblemen. It was hugely patronised by the growing upper middle class of Europeans and Indians. Their photographs, many of which were hand-tinted, comprised one of the first comprehensive archives of Indian landscapes, architecture and "types of people", becoming proud pieces of display in collectors' photo albums in the drawing rooms of the elite, both within India and abroad.

In 1874, the studio had published *Photographs of Architecture and Scenery in Gujarat and Rajputana*. Along with Lala Deen Dayal, the Bourne & Shepherd studio were one of the official photographers of the 1905 and 1911 Delhi Durbars and of the royal tour of the Prince and Princess of Wales across India through 1905–1906. The studio printed and bound a two-volume set of architectural photographs of

India, specifically for presentation to the royal couple in 1905. During the World Wars, the studio thrived on contracts for photographing Indian, British and American services personnel and their activities. The Bourne & Shepherd studio had offered technical assistance to the hugely popular Marathi film *Pundalik*, the biography of a Maharashtrian saint, directed by R.G. Torney and released at Bombay's Coronation Cinematograph in 1912.

Samuel Bourne (1834–1912), the founder-chief photographer of the studio heard about opportunities in commercial photography in India, and decided to give up his bank job in England to arrive in Calcutta in January 1863. He stayed in India for a period of seven years till 1870.

After initially photographing the Victorian buildings of the seat of the Government of British India in Calcutta, Bourne made three photographic expeditions to the Himalayas, describing them at length in the four series of letters published between 1863 and 1870 and the article "Ten weeks with a camera in the Himalayas", all published in *The British Journal of Photography*.

Samuel Bourne had been an artist before becoming a photographer and as such looked for aesthetic and technical perfection in photography, laying emphasis on colour, gradation and scale to produce "picturesque" landscape and architectural photographs, just like the Daniells had in their sketches nearly a century earlier. Bourne's landscape photographs won him medals at the Dublin and Paris International Exhibitions, and two gold medals were conferred upon him by the Bengal Photographic Society in 1865.

His first Himalayan expedition from Calcutta in 1863 was to Simla, to the higher mountain ranges beyond and to the Sutlej Valley. En route, he stopped and photographed Benares, Agra, Delhi and Ambala. He returned to Simla after ten weeks with 147 negatives of scenery that had never been photographed before at such high altitudes.

Back in Simla, Bourne partnered with the established professional photographer William Howard from Calcutta, to establish the Howard & Bourne studio. Charles Shepherd, who had been working in Agra with Arthur Robertson since 1862, joined them in 1865, and the studio was renamed Howard, Bourne & Shepherd. By 1867, Howard left the partnership and the firm flourished as Bourne & Shepherd at the "Talbot House" on the Mall. The same year, they set up a studio in Calcutta at 8, Chowringhee Road and in 1870 in Bombay at 11, Esplanade Road. The studio in Simla was operational till 1910, but all operations shifted to Calcutta thereafter.

In 1864, Samuel Bourne made his second Himalayan expedition from Lahore to the Kangra Valley and Kashmir via Byjnath, Dharamsala, Dalhousie and Chamba, which lasted nine months. On the return, he photographed the Sind Valley, Baramulla, Murree, Delhi (once again), Cawnpore (Kanpur) and Lucknow. He mentions in his letters that he was obsessed with finding water and lush vegetation for his fore and middle grounds. In this regard, what he found missing in Simla, he found in Kashmir, capturing idyllic scenes at leisure, of boats and wooden bridges over the Dal Lake. His final expedition to the hills in 1866 was a six-month long expedition and perhaps the most ambitious, in which he set out to photograph Kulu, Lahoul, Spiti, the Gangotri Glacier and Gomukh, the source of the river Ganges. On the return, he stopped and photographed Agra once more, Mussoorie, Roorkee, Meerut and Nainital. In 1868, from Calcutta, Bourne travelled to and photographed Darjeeling and other villages in Bengal. Later he went to southern India, photographing Ootacamund, the Nilgiri Hills, Tanjore and Ceylon before reaching Bombay in 1870.

Samuel Bourne was well known for travelling heavy, with a large retinue of 30–40 coolies to carry his cameras, 10-ft high portable dark room tent, chests of chemicals and glass plates, many of which would break along the way. In his letters he talks about how he had to alter the photo developing process in those early days to suit the tropical climate of India and the numerous difficult negotiations he had to do along the way with government officials and labour agents—the *chowdree*s and *lumbardar*s.

While Bourne travelled across the country pursuing landscape and architectural photography, Shepherd took charge of the studio's printing operations, of marketing Bourne's landscapes and himself executing portraitures. Between 1868 and 1875, Shepherd's portraits featured in Watson & Kaye's eight-volume publication *The People of India*. This collection of 468 photographs was one of the first major ethnographic studies to be produced by the camera.

Samuel Bourne returned to England in 1870, leaving behind his large archive of around 2,200 glass plate negatives and his photography equipment for Colin

Murray, an established professional photographer in Bombay and co-founder of the firm Saché & Murray. Murray took over the role of the travelling landscape photographer for the studio, and, eventually, the full management of the studio came to him with Charles Shepherd leaving around 1879. The photo studio operated successfully well into the 20th century, and the coveted photographs from the studio were continuously exhibited, reprinted and sold over the following years.

On returning to England in 1870, Samuel Bourne founded a very successful cotton doubling business with his brother-in-law in Nottingham, and as a hobby pursued watercolour painting. By 1874, he had withdrawn his financial interests in Bourne & Shepherd's Indian business entirely.

Bremner Photo, Lahore and Quetta (1888–1923)
Commercial Photographer

Frederick Bremner (1863–1941), the founder of Bremner Photo Studio, sailed to India from Scotland in 1883, at the age of 20, to work with his brother-in-law G.W. Lawrie at his well-established photography studio in Lucknow. Initially, Bremner worked at the numerous army cantonments in northern India photographing military men and their activities. By 1888, he had set up his own studio in Karachi, where he continued to live till the year 1892.

In 1889, soon after he started work in Karachi, Bremner was commissioned to photograph the inauguration of two major government projects — the inaugurations of the Lansdowne Bridge and the Gothic-styled Empress Market building.

After moving out of Karachi, Bremner established studios in Quetta, Lahore and Rawalpindi. For him, photography was an art, and his technically and aesthetically superior work is evident in his numerous city views, landscapes, portraitures, military and social documentaries. As an official photographer of the British Raj, Bremner's photographs capture the growing British community in the region and the establishment of their social customs and lifestyles. He had also recorded the royal tour of the Prince and Princess of Wales to the North-West Frontier Province.

Bremner worked extensively in the rarely photographed areas of Baluchistan and Sindh, at times on commission for a number of Punjabi feudal rulers. His wife assisted him with photographing the purdah-clad women.

With his reputation as a photographer established, Bremner began a successful postcard and greetings card business, publishing a wide range of photographs from all his studios. In 1910, Bremner opened a studio in Simla, the popular summer capital of the Raj. He lived there till his departure to England in 1923. Upon his return, Bremner worked on his memoir *My Forty Years in India*, which was published in the year 1940. His other works include volumes of photographs titled *Baluchistan Illustrated* (1900) and *Types of the Indian Army* (1905), which are among the only surviving photographic records of Quetta before it was destroyed by the earthquake in 1931.

S.S. Brijbasi & Sons, Karachi, Mathura and Bombay (1920s–till date)
Picture Publisher

The company was founded by the brothers Shrinathdasji and Shyamsunderlal Brijbasi at Bunder Road, Karachi, where they initially ran a picture framing shop for about five years. The idea to publish their own images was precipitated by the arrival in their shop of a Sindhi client requesting the framing of a photograph of his son dressed as Krishna, in a style similar to Krishna's representation in D.G. Phalke's 1918 film *Shree Krishna Janma*. Coincidently, earlier, a travelling sales representative from the Berlin printers Grafima visited the elder brother Shrinathdasji with a sample of prints from Germany. In 1928, the brothers decided to send to Germany, for printing, a number of original paintings by the Nathdvara artists Khubiram, Ghasiram and Narottam Narayan Sharma. Some of the paintings were close copies of the art of the Calcutta Art Studio and Ravi Varma Press lithographs. In fact, the influence from the chromolithograph landscapes and flower pictures produced by the German company L.M.B are also evident in the early Brijbasi prints. While the original paintings were mostly 10 x 14 inch, they were reproduced as postcard-size (3½ x 5 in) bromide prints. The prints were of highly superior quality, printed on thick and glossy paper, in attractive colours with wonderful brightness. This first set of bromide postcard designs was registered in Calcutta in July 1928 and began to be widely used for correspondence, making the products hugely successful in the niche postcard markets. This was despite the tough competition posed by the technically superior colour lithographs coming from the Ravi Varma Press, amongst others.

The gouaches for printing were sent from India by Brijbasi and the initial print runs ranged between one and five thousand in the first few years, with reprint orders going as high as ten thousand by 1937. The title of the picture was printed along with the S.S. Brijbasi logo and the inscription "Printed in Germany". With supplies from Germany being suspended during the War, Brijbasi's images were printed in Nagpur and Bombay, each picture carrying the phrase "Printed as German".

Lal Chand & Sons, Delhi (Est. 1921)
Commercial Photographer

Based out of Dariba in Delhi, Lal Chand & Sons photographed the monuments and people of the North Indian cities of Delhi, Agra and Lucknow. Their photographs were used for finely printed black-and-white collotype postcards that were printed in Saxony. The postcards of Delhi and Agra were put together as albums and were popularly sold as tourist guides, and were used in later-day travel books as well.

Chitrashala Steam Press, Poona (Est. 1878)
Printer and Publisher

Closely linked to the Indian nationalist movement and, at times, the revolutionary movement of Western India, Chitrashala Press was founded in 1878 by Vishnu Krishna Chiplunkar (1850–1882), in partnership with Balkrishna Pant Joshi and Shankar Tukaram Shahigram. Chiplunkar was an exemplary personality who in his short life had a deep influence on the nationalist thinking of Bal Gangadhar Tilak.

Chiplunkar established two printing presses: the Arya Bhushan for printing Tilak's newspapers *Kesari* and *Mahratta*; and the Chitrashala, for encouraging fine arts, viewing publication of journals and of chromolithographs as complimentary activities. Earlier, in 1874, Chiplunkar had started an influential literary and political magazine—*Nibandha Mala*.

The earliest print issued by Chitrashala Press was of Nana Phadnavis, a heroic figure for Chitpavan Brahmans such as Tilak and Chiplunkar. However, the first commercial success for the printing press came with the Hindu mythological print *Rampanchayatam*, based on a painting made in 1874. Chitrashala sold two thousand copies of this print in a month and followed this up by *Shivpanchayatam*.

Following the success of these prints, Chitrashala produced more than a hundred large-format coloured lithographs of Hindu mythological deities that were appealing to Indians across north and western India. These images clearly marked the impact of the "single point perspective", incorporating life-study drawings and exotic "European Looking Landscapes", a hallmark of printed images of gods at that time.

In the wake of the 1910 Press Act, that intensified state surveillance of visual and written texts, Chitrashala Press used images on postcards to covertly further their anti-colonial propaganda. They printed images of decorative caged and uncaged parrots on postcards to be widely used by the public. Probably owing to this political antagonism to the colonial rule, Chitrashala Press was largely marginalised in colonial narratives, much in contrast to Ravi Varma Press' appeal to his colonial patrons. Chiplunkar's death in 1882 led to the newly appointed manager buying over the shares of the two other partners. The functioning of the press continued well into the 20th century.

Clifton & Co., Bombay (1896/7–1930s)
Commercial Photographer and Publisher

Harry Clifton Soundy, the founder of the studio, was born in Bombay in 1863. A skilled watercolourist, Harry worked as a manager for the Bourne & Shepherd's Bombay studio at Esplanade Road, from 1889 to 1894. He founded Clifton & Co. around 1896. Initially Harry Clifton worked out of a studio at Meadows Street, Bombay, which was a venue for daily screenings of silent films. Eventually, he moved to Albert Building at Hornby Road. Over time, the studio built a huge photo archive of Bombay.

Between 1899–1901, the national daily *The Times of India* carried several advertisements and news clips featuring Clifton's photographs and postcards. These capture British Indian life such as the Presidency Cricket Match, Bombay Volunteer Rifles Cycling Club, hunting, yachting and Indian Christmas cards.

In January 1900, Clifton & Co. had placed an advertisement to buy a new or second-hand collotype printing press, indicating their expansion and growth in the city of Bombay. In fact, the studio became one of India's first few printers of complex collotype postcards featuring topographical views and native people across various professions. This marked the transition from lithographic and artist-drawn images to photographs as the primary source for Indian postcards.

Clifton & Co. became a popular provider of colourful postcards, recording the transformation of Bombay from a harbour into a large merchant town. The studio's photographs were used in Playne's *The Bombay Presidency (1918–1920)*, a voluminous book surveying businesses across the Raj.

Besides publishing their own images, the studio also published images for photographers like Fred Bremner.

In his personal life, Harry Clifton had married in Mussoorie and lived with his family at 17, Harkness Road, Malabar Hill. After his death in 1922 at St. George's Hospital, Bombay, he was buried in Sewree Cemetery. His wife Daisy was recorded as proprietress of the business up until 1933.

The Collectors' Publishing Company, London (1900–1907)
Publisher

During the early years of the picture postcard boom, the Collectors' Publishing Company came out with the magazine *The Picture Postcard*, in the interest of the growing number of postcard collectors. They also became postcard agent of many other publishers. The firm used the logo "Mercury Series" on their postcards and their magazine cover, and is known to have published several topographical postcards of London and the other cities of the British Empire. Their office was situated at 42/44, Imperial Buildings, Ludgate Circus.

A.J. Combridge & Co., Madras and Bombay (Est. late 19th century)
Publisher and Bookseller

A.J. Combridge & Co. acted as agent for the sale of publications issued by the Central Provinces Government. Their postcards appeared in the early 1900s and included topographical views of Indian cities, government buildings, rituals, festivals and the Indian royalty. The German photographers Wiele & Klein sold the right to publish their prints to A.J. Combridge and Co.

The firm had offices in England and Ireland as well.

S.H. Dagg, Allahabad and Mussoorie (Est. 1890s/early 1900s)
Photographic Artist

S.H. Dagg extensively photographed Mussoorie and its surrounding landscapes. He also photographed buildings of Lucknow, Allahabad, Benares and Delhi. Several portraits are also attributed to Dagg. All of his postcards were printed in Germany.

Hernam Dass & Sons, Ambala and Dagshai (Est. late 19th century)
Publisher

Hernam Dass & Sons' postcards appear as early as the 1880s and continue till the early 1900s. Most of their postcards are of the cities of Punjab, and were printed in Germany.

Moorli Dhur & Sons, Ambala (Est. 1899)
Publisher

Moorli Dhur & Sons was a prominent Indian publishing house, situated in Sudder Bazar, producing postcards of India and of regions that are now in Pakistan. The firm's thematic areas were railways, topography, military and architecture. The postcards published ranged from black-and-white to tinted collotypes and also a distinctive range with a green border and gold decoration. Their postcards were printed in Germany and Great Britain.

M.V. Dhurandhar, Bombay (1867–1944)
Artist

Born in Kohlapur, Maharashtra, Dhurandhar was one of the first students at the J.J. School of Arts, where he later taught and went on to become the head of institute. He evolved as a remarkable artist, and his work was characterised with profound realism. Dhurandhar was one of the first great Indian artists to create a series of around 70 postcards between 1900 and 1905, at a time when postcards had just begun to appear internationally. He is best known for postcards depicting the modernisation of his city, Bombay, its ethnic diversity and the portraits of its new wealthy merchants. *The Marwari Woman* is one of his most popular paintings. Some of his postcards were published by the firm owned by Dadasaheb Phalke.

Dias & Co., Mahableshwar (Late 19th century–20th century)
Photographic Studio
The studio published reprographic prints of Mahableshwar on postcards, several being hand-tinted. Their postcards were printed in Germany.

A. Hajee Dossul & Sons, Karachi (1840–1900s)
Publishers
Located at Elphinstone Street, A. Hajee Dossul & Sons was a prominent publisher of picture postcards of Pakistani cities. Most of their black-and-white picture postcards capture the modernisation and growth of the city of Karachi. The firm also dealt in general merchandise, fancy goods and ammunition.

A. Druet
Artist
A. Druet is a French artist whose paintings were used in postcards in the early 20th century.

Dutta, Kashmir
Commercial Photographer
Many picturesque postcards of Kashmir are attributed to Dutta. All his postcards were numbered.

Byramjee Eduljee, Karachi
Commercial Photographer
Eduljee was a reputed commercial photographer based in Karachi. He was one of the few photographers whose name appeared in the postcards that featured his photographs.

Ali Mahomed Fazal, Bombay (Early 1900s)
Publisher
Ali Mahomed Fazal published black-and-white postcards of Bombay and other cities, including Mt. Abu. The postcards were largely printed in Germany.

Edicao de Christovam Fernandes, Nova Goa (Early 1900s)

Several Goa postcards were published in the Christovam Fernandes Edition. The subjects included views of Goa, portraits of its people and details of its churches.

Ludwig Hans Fischer (1848–1915)
Artist (Painter)

Ludwig Hans Fischer was an Austrian landscape painter and etcher. He studied at the Vienna Academy of Fine Arts. Later, he travelled and painted extensively in Italy, Spain, North Africa, Egypt and India before settling in Vienna. Many of his paintings were printed as postcards. His prominent work in Vienna includes the execution of nine decorative landscapes for the Vienna Museum of Natural History in 1889. Among his series of etchings and engravings, *Historical Landscapes from Austria-Hungary* is the most remarkable production.

Fitch & Co.
Retailer and Distributor

A popular supermarket of Mussoorie, Fitch & Co. retailed postcards of Mussoorie and Landour that were published abroad.

G.L.N.C
Commercial Photographer

Although the full name of this photographer is not known, the numerous photographs of Simla taken by G.L.N.C were used extensively by the publisher Moorli Dhur & Sons.

Nestor Gianaclis Ltd, Calcutta (Pre-1914)
Publisher

Nestor published a wide range of fine postcards containing views of Calcutta, Meerut, Agra, Benares and Lahore. The postcards captured the daily life and rituals of the local people. The company also published several portraits. Many of the postcards were coloured and embossed. All their postcards were printed in Germany and were numbered.

M. Gilbert. Galland (1920s)
Artist

M. Gilbert Galland was a French artist known for his aquarells that were used as French maritime art postcards of countries such as India, Egypt, Algeria, Istanbul and China. His art was also reproduced as travel posters and advertisements.

M.M. Gargh & Co., Agra
Publisher

Printed postcards of Delhi, Kanpur and Agra. The back of their postcards indicate "Universal Postal Union – British India", and were printed in Germany.

Ghosal Bros, Shillong
Publisher

Ghosal Bros published divided-back postcards of Shillong, capturing the city's prominent landmarks.

Gobindram Oodeyram, Jaipur (1880s–1970s)
Commercial Photographer

For over a century, the father and son duo Gobindram and Oodeyram ran an eminent studio in Jaipur. They established connection with the photo studio of their late King Ram Singh II. Thereafter, they did extensive work photographing women of the court and people with different professions, akin to the Company School Art. Some of their published postcards, like those of the Maharaja of Jaipur and his family, were lightly hand-coloured. Given their proximity to the Maharaja, Gobindram Oodeyram photographed several visiting dignitaries. In 1890, they created a leather-bound album to commemorate the visit of Archduke Ferdinand of Austria.

Guerra & Sons, Mhow (WWI and after)
Publisher

The postcards of Guerra & Sons, situated at 107 Post Office Road, carried images of the Mhow Cantonment and the countryside around.

A. Haq & Sons, Benares
Publisher

A. Haq published divided-back postcards of the Benares ghats, the day-to-day activities around it, and of Sarnath.

Dinshaw H. Hazary, Ootacamund
Publisher

Hazary was a prominent publisher of a large number of collotype postcards of scenes from the Nilgiris during the 1930s–1940s.

Higginbotham & Co., Madras and Bangalore (Est. 1844)
Bookseller, Publisher and Stationer

Higginbotham is the oldest surviving bookshop of India and was established by an English librarian named Abel Joshua Higginbotham, who had arrived in India as a British stowaway! In the 1840s, he started working at the Weslyan Book Shop in Madras that was run by Protestant missionaries. In 1844, when the bookshop ran into heavy losses, Higginbotham purchased the business at a relatively low price and named it Higginbotham's.

By the 1850s, Higginbotham became well-regarded and hugely popular with his customers and the store had established its reputation as a premier bookshop of Madras. The shop's inventory grew and in the 1860s, the store started stocking stationery as well, and also started publishing their own books. Higginbotham's also became the official book supplier to the government, and was appointed as "Booksellers to His Royal Highness" during the visit of the Prince of Wales to Madras in 1875. On Abel's death in 1891, his son C.H. Higginbotham took over and expanded the business beyond Madras. He established bookstalls at many railway stations of southern India. In 1904, the diamond jubilee of the establishment, Higginbotham's moved to a new building, specifically built to meet their growing business needs. The high ceiling allowed the air to circulate in order to reduce mustiness which could harm the books. The warehouse and printing press were also part of the building where they continue to operate even today. By 1929, the firm had as many as 400 employees.

Higginbotham's published the landmark "Guide to Madras" and also began printing picture postcards of the sights and scenes of Madras, the Nilgiris and Bangalore during the period 1910–1920.

In 1921, Spencer's acquired Higginbotham's, and in 1945 the management of the bookstore and its printing press was taken over by the Amalgamations Group.

Joseph Hoffmann/Joseph (Jos) Heim, Vienna (1831–1904)
Artist/Publisher

The career of the Viennese prodigious artist Joseph Hoffmann began with an exhibition at the age of fifteen. Later, he studied briefly at the Viennese Academy. Like many European artists at that time, Hoffmann travelled to Persia and India in 1850 in search of inspiration. After returning from India the following year, he worked for a well-known Viennese studio. Later, Hoffmann settled down to a career exclusively as a historical landscape painter. In April 1898, a series of "Artists Postcards" by Hoffmann were published by Joseph Heim (possibly a pseudonym used by Joseph Hoffmann for his commercial efforts) in Vienna. This was the time when illustrated postcards had just begun to appear. Hoffmann's series included three postcards of Benares, two of Jaipur, and one each of Gwalior, Bombay and Hyderabad. These postcards had been printed from Hoffmann's richly colored aquarells. An advertisement in the second issue of the Viennese postcard collectors' journal *Die Illustrierte Postkarte* (*The Illustrated Postcard*) included this series. Hoffmann's postcards were amongst the first postcards of India to be signed by the artist and were posted all across the world as early as 1899. His postcards were sold by Thacker, Spink & Co., the largest retailer of postcards during the British Raj.

Holmes, Peshawar (First half of the 20th century)
Commercial Photographer/Artist

Randolph Bezant Holmes (1888–1973) established the R.B. Holmes & Co. photography studio in Peshawar, Pakistan. He was one of the official photographers of the Afghan Wars in the North-West Frontier region of Afghanistan. One of his best works is his coverage of the 3rd Afghan War in 1919.

Holmes also spent some time in Kashmir. As part of his documentary and surveillance work, Holmes extensively photographed the large British military camps and towers in the region, the characteristic landscapes dotted with camel caravans and military convoys, the villages and religious structures. Several of the photographs were hand-tinted, probably by him.

A fine artist, Holmes executed several individual portraits and watercolour landscapes of the areas that he had earlier photographed. In 1929 he published a memoir of his time in Afghanistan titled *Story of the North West Frontier Province,* containing gelatin print plates of his landscapes.

Johnston & Hoffmann, Calcutta (1880–1950s)
Commercial Photographer and Publisher

Established in 1880 by P.A. Johnston and Theodore Julius Hoffmann at 22, Chowringhee Road, Calcutta, the firm came to be one of the finest commercial studios and photographic publishers in India. Their photographs captured everyday street scenes, daily occupations and classical architecture, rarely focussing on iconic views that were associated with tourist postcards. Very often employed by the British merchants of Calcutta, Johnston & Hoffman provided studies of the teak, jute and tea industries. They had also produced a series of archaeological photographs that the Encyclopedia Britannica still makes use of, after more than 100 years since they were taken.

From around 1890, Hoffmann maintained a studio in Darjeeling, and shorter-lived studios at Simla and Rangoon. The studio is well known for their photographs of the characteristic "types" of people from north and North-East India, Burma and Sri Lanka. The studio was commissioned by the famous English antiquarian, scholar and explorer Lieutenant Colonel L.A. Waddell to take portraits of "Types of Natives of Nepal, Sikkim & Tibet". Many of the full face and profile portraits were published in Waddell's *Among the Himalayas* (1889). In time, the album became part of the Royal Anthropological Institute Photographic Collection.

Johnston and Hoffmann photographed all the principal events of the 1905-1906 India tour of the Prince and Princess of Wales, including the interior and exterior views of the royal train, which was specially built to carry the

Prince and Princess. The royal tour souvenir album contained 19 images. Thereafter the studio also recorded the second royal tour and Delhi Durbar in 1911–1912.

By 1910, under the management of A. D. Long, the firm's catalogue rivaled that of Bourne & Shepherd. Johnston & Hoffmann became one of the longest-surviving studios in the subcontinent and continued to function under Indian management into the early 1950s.

G.K. Husain & Co., Jubbulpore (Early 1900s)
Publisher
The company, situated in Sadar Bazar, published postcards of Jubbulpore with images of the city's landmarks, merchants and the marble rocks. Most of their postcards were numbered.

P.S. Joshi, Bombay
Publisher
Located in Ghatkopar, they were publishers of postcards with views of Bombay and the paintings of Raja Ravi Varma.

Joshi Bros, Bombay (1910)
Picture Merchant
Situated at 221, Bazargate Street, they were publishers of art postcards by artists such as M.V. Dhurandhar and Raja Ravi Varma, depicting scenes from Indian mythology.

P.D. Kapoor & Sons, Peshawar (1930s)
Photographer and Publisher
Numerous black-and-white "Real Photo Picture Postcards" of the people and views of the NWFP region have been photographed and published by P.D. Kapoor & Sons.

Ahmed Kasim & Co., Poona (Early 1900s)
Publisher

Ahmed Kasim & Co. published topographical postcards of several Indian cities such as Poona, Ahmedabad, Jaipur, Calcutta, Bombay and Madras. Some of their postcards dating to pre-1907 have undivided backs. The name of the publisher was often rubber stamped at the back of postcards, and most of them were printed in Saxony.

J&H King, Simla (1905–1910)
Commercial Photographer

This relatively lesser-known studio produced work of high quality. Views of Simla, Dharmasala and the album with 49 images recording the December 1905 Rawalpindi Manoeuvres are attributed to J&H King.

Jadu Kissen, Delhi (1910–1920s)
Commercial Photographer

Jadu Kissen is best known for his "Archeological Series" that captured historic landmarks. He turned many of his images into black-and-white, monotone, and tinted collotype postcards. He founded the studio The Arch Photo-Works of India at Kashmere Gate, Delhi. Numerous postcards of Simla, Kashmir and Delhi were published from this studio.

Kosmos, Budapest, Hungary (1890s)
Publisher

Kosmos published numerous undivided-back topographical postcards of several Asian, American and European cities. Their postcards were produced using the chromolithograph technique, usually with a limited pallet. They also produced a few "hold to light" cards. Kosmos also had an office in Munich, probably where their cards may have been printed. Some postcards are believed to have been produced in conjunction with Emil Storch in Vienna.

Priya Lall/K. Lall & Co., Agra (1878–till date)
Publisher, Photographer and Dealer

A large number of photographs and postcards of the monuments and the life of the people of Agra are attributed to this photography studio. Several of their images of Agra were presented to the Queen of England and the studio was rewarded with a gold medal during the British Raj. Around 1931, they also published a pictorial guide book of Agra with 25 half-tone pictures, clicked by Priya Lall, of the city's monuments and their brief histories. The studio operates out of several Indian cities even today and has earned the distinction of having photographed several political leaders and celebrities during the British Raj and post Independence.

M. Lescuyer, Lyon (Early 20th century)
Printer

Lescuyer, situated at 16, r. des Remparts-d'Ainay, printed postcards of Bombay, China and the French colonies in Africa for the benefit of the Salesian and Jesuit Missions of Lyon, and also for the "Missions Africaines". Some of their postcards were sepia-toned. They also printed some religious books.

The Locomotive Magazine Series, London (1897–1950s)
Artist and Publisher

The Locomotive Magazine was published by The Locomotive Publishing Company, specialising in railway images, especially locomotives. The publishing company was one of the first picture stock libraries to make railway photographs commercially available. Their archive included images of light, narrow gauge and industrial railways. Railway photography was increasing in popularity in the beginning of the 20th century; the number of photographers grew and demand for their work from groups of railway collectors and enthusiasts was at its peak.

The archive and publishing house was started as a hobby in the 1890s by two railway enthusiasts—the brothers A.R. Bell and A. Morton Bell, while they worked as apprentices with the Great Eastern Railway at Stratford. They traded under the name *F. Moore's Railway Photographs* to conceal their connections with the GER.

A third brother, Walter John Bell, and another apprentice, A.C.W. Lowe, joined them in 1896 and together they launched *Moore's Monthly Magazine*, the first ever railway periodical. Its popularity grew, and from the 13th issue in January 1897, the magazine was renamed *The Locomotive Magazine*.

The Locomotive Publishing Company was formally registered in 1899. The company drew on an archive of railway images that the Bell brothers had acquired over the years working at the GER, from the steadily growing band of amateur, official and commissioned railway photographers. The business greatly expanded during the first decades of the 20th century. LPC initially issued its photographs as 10 x 8 and 8½ x 6½ inch prints or as "cartes de visites", but in the early 1900s the company started catering to the new postcard-collecting hobby and sold large quantities of photographs as postcards, particularly as themed sets. The increase in mass holidays and excursions, which itself was propelled by the expanding railway network, further increased the use of these postcards. Some postcards, particularly the more populist photographs, were coloured.

John Rudd, another artist working under the "F Moore" pseudonym, painted oil pictures of locomotives and trains for over 40 years, leaving behind an incomparable collection of all forms of the railways available those days. Colour plates of his paintings were produced for *The Locomotive Magazine* from 1897 until 1933. He is best known for the series of coloured postcards which appeared between 1903 and 1927. Many reprints followed later. His paintings were also used in other railway magazines and books, and also for cigarette cards.

The publishing company survived the London bombing during the Second World War and was sold in 1951 to publisher Ian Allan. In 1992, the archive, together with its associated rights, was acquired by the National Railway Museum, with the assistance of the National Heritage Memorial Fund. They are still registered as a dormant company.

D. Macropolo & Co. Ltd, Calcutta (1920–1979)
Publisher

D. Macropolo & Co. was a well-known publisher of black-and-white as well as hand-coloured collotype postcards depicting local views and street life of various

Indian cities. Some of their cards were printed on glossy paper and they resembled hand-coloured photographs. Macropolo's postcards were printed both in Germany and England. By 1942 they ventured into the then profitable cigarette industry, and were purchased by Philip Morris through Godfrey Philips in 1979.

Shriniwas Mahadeo & Sons, Belgaum (Est. late 19th century) and Bangalore (Est. 1903)
Photographer

Srinivas Mahadeo Welling, a native of the Goan village of Velling, received a camera as a gift and decided to venture into independent professional photography in the 1850s. He travelled across the country taking pictures and lugging his heavy equipment on a bullock cart even as far as Karachi.

Mahadeo's son, Govind Srinivas, set up the family's first photo studio called "Welling Camera Works" in Belgaum. They also manufactured cameras till the Second World War. Mahadeo's grandson, Gajanan Govind Welling, was the first to venture into creative photography and became well known as a portrait artist. His artistic execution and superior print quality made him very popular. G.G. Welling participated in exhibitions abroad, winning numerous awards. His pictures were also featured in the *The Royal Photographic Society Journal,* of which he had been a member. The Wellings had photographed the sages Ramana Maharishi and Swami Vivekananda. One of the most famous close-up photographs of Ramana Maharishi taken by G.G. Welling around the year 1948 has been titled the "Welling Bust".

In 1945, G.G. Welling, along with his son S.G. Welling, became founding members of the Mysore Photographic Society, and they continued to support it actively. S.G. Welling focussed on architectural and topographical photography in Karnataka well into the 1980s.

Mahatta & Co., Srinagar, Delhi (1912–till date)
Commercial Photographer and Publisher

The famous photography studio was started by the brothers Amar Nath Mehta and Ram Chand Mehta in 1912 as Mehta & Co. They began from a houseboat on the river Jhelum in Srinagar, but by 1918 they moved the studio to the Jhelum

Bund. R.C. Mehta stayed as the photographer and the other brothers managed the other functions of the studio.

The studio's prime location and its proximity to the British Residency and the Post Office ensured a fairly large clientele of the city's elite, especially for self-portraits. The studio was appointed official photographer of the state for a while. Over time, the studio came to be called "Mahatta & Co." by, mainly, its British clientele, who couldn't pronounce the founders' surname—Mehta.

With postcards gaining popularity, R.C. Mehta travelled across the valley photographing the panoramic views, people and their daily life. The studio printed beautiful black-and-white/colour postcards of Kashmir. All their postcards were printed in Saxony and were numbered. Even now, the studio has an archive of around 7,000 images of the valley from the period between 1934 to 1965. Today, they continue to enlarge and process these archival prints in high quality. They have also published a booklet titled "Srinagar Views 1934–65".

As the business flourished, Mahatta & Co. opened branches in Gulmarg, Nagin, Murree, Lahore and Rawalpindi. After Partition, the Lahore and Muree shops shut down, though the Rawalpindi shop continued to operate for a few years. Apart from the studio at Srinagar, which is still functioning, the other studios and shops in the valley closed down gradually.

During the 1970s and 80s, patrons of Mahatta & Sons were prominent political families and popular Hindi-film stars. The studio developed and printed still photos used for advertising the numerous films that were shot in Kashmir.

The studio in Srinagar still retains the old-world charm with its display of old pictures of Kashmir of the 1930s and 1940s. The wood-and-glass cabinets still house antique camera equipment, accessories and old records that were meticulously stored by R.C. Mehta.

Over time, the Mehtas set up a studio at Connaught Place in Delhi, which is still in operation. Madan Mahatta, one of the descendants of the family was the first Indian photographer to have studied at the Guilford School of Arts and Crafts, Surrey, England. Upon his return to India in 1954, he was commissioned by the first generation of Indian architects, trained under Walter Gropius & Frank Llyod Wright, to photograph the first modern urban planning in India—

the "Master Urban Plan, DDA, 1962", which took place under the supervision of Albert Mayer. His fine architectural photographs, the "Delhi Modern Architecture Series", span over 30 years (1950s–1980s) and document the interplay of form, function and aesthetics.

T. Mamundy Pillay & Sons, Bangalore
Publisher

Publisher of embossed and black-and-white postcards of Bangalore and Madras. Many of their postcards were published in Prussia.

Mela Ram & Sons, Peshawar (First half of 20th century–till date)
Commercial Photographer

Along with Holmes and K.C. Mehra, Mela Ram's photographs are among the rare images of the North-West Frontier Province taken during the Raj. As a pioneering war photographer, Mela Ram accompanied the British army, photographing their military expeditions in the Frontier during the 1920s and 1930s. Some of his portraits of British soldiers photographed with props in the background were printed as Cabinet Cards.

Mela Ram also photographed the Hijrat Movement of August 1920, when more than thirty thousand Muslims from Punjab and the NWFP decided to migrate to the nearest Muslim country, Afghanistan, in protest of the aggressive policies of the British government and for the restoration of the Ottoman Empire.

Though Mela Ram himself never came to India, his eldest son Labindranath and his three grandsons—Roshan Lall, Hiral Lall and Kishan Lall—migrated to Dehradun with a battalion of the 5th Gorkha Rifles and set up a studio there in 1947. Currently the photo studio is the official photographer of the Doon School.

H.A. Mirza & Sons, Delhi (1907–1912)
Commercial Photographer and Publisher

Based in Chandni Chowk, Delhi, H.A. Mirza & Sons produced a large number of picture postcards of Delhi's Islamic monuments and colonial landmarks. Their photographs were mostly devoid of the city people and focussed on the symmetry and harmony of the Islamic architecture. Besides photographing Indian cities, the studio published 14 views of Mecca and Medina on 15 October 1907. These were published both as photographs and postcards. Mirza also photographed several other places across Southeast Asia. All their postcards were printed in Germany.

Rewachand Motumul & Sons, Karachi
Publisher

A large number of topographical postcards of Karachi published during the period 1911–13 are attributed to this publisher.

W. Newman & Co. Ltd, Calcutta (Late 19th century–1960s)
Bookseller, Stationer and Printer

Published a large number of fine topographical postcards of Calcutta dating back to the early 1900s. The firm also published views of the landscapes of Darjeeling. A well-known Delhi postcard published by Newman & Co. in 1910 features a street scene with Jama Masjid in the background. Some of their early postcards were sepia-toned or lithographed. Both their divided- and undivided-back postcards were published as "copyright postcards", part of the "Dalhousie Series", and carried their characteristic logo on the back. All their postcards were printed in England.

The firm, situated at 3, Old Court House Street, remained a prominent publisher of atlases, travel guide books, books on history and other subjects till the 1960s.

Nissim Bros, Calcutta
Publisher

Nissim Brothers published numerous divided-back postcards of Calcutta.

Omed Singh & Pyarey Lall, Delhi
Publisher

Omed Singh & Pyarey Lall, a Delhi-based studio, published several views of Delhi on postcards including details of the Red Fort, Jama Masjid and views of the Kashmere Gate. All postcards had a serial number and were printed by Dott. A. Baggio & Co., Torino, Italy.

Orbis Publishing House, Prague (Early 1900s)
Publisher

A Czech publishing house that published numerous picture postcards of a number of cities across the world and also a large array of books.

The Oriental Commercial Bureau, Calcutta (1910)
Publisher

The Oriental Commercial Bureau, situated at 31, Elliot Lane, published numerous divided-back and black-and-white postcards of Calcutta.

A.H. Perris & Co., Calcutta (Early 20th century)
Publisher

Perris & Co. published numerous embossed topographical postcards of the city of Calcutta between the period 1910–15. These divided-back postcards were printed in Great Britain and Saxony.

The Phototype Company, Bombay (Early 1900s)
Publisher

A large Indian publisher of black-and-white postcards, with subjects ranging from city views to people and their professions. Most of their postcards were printed in Germany and Luxembourg.

The Picture House, Bangalore
Publisher

The Picture House, situated in 3, Brigade Road, published divided-back and black-and-white postcards of Bangalore in the early 1900s.

The Picturesque India Series, The International P.P.C Club, Allahabad
Around the year 1908, postcards of Jaipur and Agra were printed as part of this series.

R. W. Rai & Sons, Quetta
Publisher

A publishing house based in Quetta, R.W. Rai & Sons published several postcards of the sights and people of Baluchistan. They also republished many of the popular sepia postcards of the prominent photographer K.C. Marrott, who ran his own studio in Karachi in the early 1900s.

M. Rathnam & Co., Vizag
Publisher

M. Rathnam & Co. published divided-back coloured postcards of Vizag.

Reynolds & Co., The Mall Pharmacy, Nainital
Publisher

Reynolds & Co. published postcards of Nainital and its surroundings. All their postcards were printed in England.

W. Roessler, Calcutta (Late 19th century–early 20th century)
Artist, Commercial Photographer and Postcard Publisher

W. Roessler was an Austrian artist, photographer and postcard publisher living in Calcutta. He published one of the earliest postcards of Calcutta. Most of these were in the "Gruss aus" (Greetings from) format. All of Roessler's postcards were printed in Austria. His oldest postcard was postally used sometime around 1897.

Thomas & Julian Rust, Allahabad, Mussoorie, Landour and Meerut (1874–1930s)
Art Photographers

The father and son duo from Italy were well known for their art landscapes and portraits taken in the lesser Himalayan region. During 1870–74, Thomas Rust, the father, ran the Calcutta Photographic Company with W.T. Burgess. In 1874, Rust opened his own studios in Allahabad, Mussoorie, Murree, Landour and Meerut. His son Julian joined the firm in 1899 and continued to manage it till 1930.

Saeed Bros, Benares (Mid-1890s onwards)
Commercial Photographer and Publisher

A prominent photo studio of Benares and publisher of numerous picture postcards of the city, their postcards depicted views of the city's ghats, temples and the various rituals of the sages and fakirs that fascinated the westerners. All their postcards were printed in Germany. Three lavishly illustrated books on Benares published in the early 1900s, namely, E.B. Havell's *Benares, The Sacred City: Sketches of Hindu Life and Religion* (1905), Rev. C. Phillips Cape's *Benares: The Stronghold of Hinduism* (1908) and Edwin Greaves' *Kashi: The City Illustrious* (1909), contain numerous pictures supplied by the Saeed Bros studio. Their postcards continued to appear well into the 1920s. The studio also published a few postcards of Darjeeling.

Parsi Sah, Nainital
Commercial Photographer

Sah photographed Nainital in the early 1900s.

Carnatic Studio, P.S. Sastri & Co., Madras
Publisher

Published black-and-white postcards of Madras. Their postcards were numbered, and were published in Saxony.

J. Serravallo, Trieste, Italy (Early 20th century)
Chemist and Publisher

J. Serravallo was a manufacturing chemist, well known for his "Serravallo's Tonic". They were also a large publisher of art and advertisement postcards, and postcards of topographical views of cities in Europe and Asia.

J. Shapoorjee & Co., Allahabad and Nainital (Early 1900s)
Publisher

The firm published several postcards featuring the architecture of Allahabad and Nainital. Most of their postcards were numbered.

Shunker Dass & Co., Lahore (Early 1900s)
Publisher

Shunker Dass & Co. was one of the largest distributors of imported postcards within India. They published a large number of black-and-white postcards of the city of Lahore, which were printed in Saxony.

Lal Singh & Co., Amritsar (Interwar period)
Publisher

Lal Singh & Co. published black-and-white topographical postcards of the city of Amritsar.

Societa Editrice Cartoline, Torino (Society of Postcard Publishing, Turin)
Publisher

They published a wide range of topographical postcards of several cities around the world.

Souza & Paul Fotografos, Nova Goa (1920s)
Publisher

Souza and Paul published postcards of the numerous historic sights and panoramic views of Goa.

Spencer & Co., Madras (Est. 1864)
Departmental Store/Publisher

The store J.W. Spencer opened in Madras in 1864 and grew into one of the largest departmental stores in Asia. After becoming a limited company in 1897, they began to publish tinted halftone postcards of views of Madras and Bangalore, and types of people and occupations, which were some of the earliest undivided back-postcards (pre-1907) of this region.

M.L. Sugan Chand, Delhi
Photographer

A Delhi-based photographer, Sugan Chand's photographs were published as postcards by Raphael Tuck & Sons.

D.B. Taraporevala & Sons, Bombay (1864–till date)
Publisher, Bookseller, News Agent and Stationer

One of the oldest and most prominent publishers of their time, Taraporevala & Sons was located at 210, Hornby Road, Fort, Mumbai. They were agents for the sale of publications issued by the Central Provinces Government. The firm produced a large number of topographic postcards, mostly of Bombay and also of other cities such as Lucknow and Ootacamund. Also attributed to this firm are lithographic postcards of people and their professions, including works of the prominent Bombay artist M.V. Dhurandhar. Many of their postcards were printed in Germany under the title "Taraporevala Elite Series", and were numbered. The firm received the warrant of "By Appointment to H.E. the Marquees of Linlithgow, Viceroy & Governor-General of India". D.B. Taraporevala & Sons continue to be book publishers even now.

Thacker, Spink & Co., Calcutta/Thacker & Co., Bombay (1853–1960)
Publisher, Stationer and Bookseller

A prominent publisher of literature and history books, and guides and almanacs, the firm was appointed as the agents for the sale of publications of the Central Provinces Government. Between the years 1864 to 1884, they published the Bengal Directory, covering the Bengal Presidency, including present-day Myanmar and Bangladesh. 1885 onwards, their directory covered the entire British India and was renamed "Thacker's Indian Directory". Once postcards were introduced in British India, Thacker & Co. became one of the early publishers and largest retailers of picture postcards. Most of their postcards were published in Saxony and Great Britain. Their distribution office in London was W. Thacker & Co. at 2, Creed Lane, and Calcutta office was situated at 3, Esplanade East.

Raphael Tuck & Sons, London (Est. 1866)
Printer and Publisher

Raphael Tuch/Tuck, born in East Prussia in 1821, moved to London in 1865 with his wife and seven children. He had a flair for commercial art, and in October 1866, Tuck opened a small shop in London, selling furniture and picture frames. He would carry his wares around the streets of London in a hand cart. By 1870, his three sons—Adolph, Herman and Gustave—joined him in importing and publishing oleographs and photographs. In 1871, they published their first set of Christmas greetings card. Amidst strong competition from the well-established printers and publishers of continental Europe, Raphael Tuck took his firm towards becoming the foremost fine art publishers of Great Britain. The firm's distinctive trademark of an easel, palette and brushes and the monogram "R.T & S." was registered in 1881. The trademark appeared on both the front and back (in the space designated for the stamp) of their postcards.

In 1893, the firm received the "Royal Warrant of Appointment to Her Majesty the Queen", a distinction which they continued to win through each succeeding reign. This insignia was stamped on all their postcards. Interestingly, at some time, Sir Arthur Conan Doyle became a part of the Tuck Board of Directors!

The firm started publishing small-size picture postcards in 1894. For the next four years, Raphael Tuck pursued with the post office to introduce full-size postcards in Great Britain, which were eventually allowed from the year 1899. Largely, Raphael Tuck & Sons published postcards of the numerous sights of England; the kings and queens; illustrations of the works of British writers, poets and artists; jokes and puzzles and so on.

"Tuck & Sons' Proof" series were printed on superior board, and every set was stamped with a consecutive number. A register was maintained to keep a track of the sale of these sets.

By 1903, the "Oilette" postcard series was introduced which came to account for about 80 per cent of their postcard sales. These postcards were high-quality colour prints of oil paintings created by a group of acclaimed artists employed by the company. From 1905 onwards, the Oilette range included themes from all over the globe in the "Wide-Wide-World" Series.

Numerous postcards on India were printed in the various geographic and thematic series. Notable amongst these was the set "Native Life in India" by the Australian painter Mortimer Menpes. Menpes toured India in 1902–03, capturing the colourful density of Indian scenes. He often painted like an outsider, with his characters having their backs to the viewer with few facial features visible.

Tuck & Sons also published postcards with topographical photographs taken by the Delhi-based M.L. Sugan Chand. Karachi-based S.J. Co-operative Society was the sole agent designated for selling Tuck postcards throughout India through several outlets.

All Tuck & Sons' postcards came with detailed descriptive captions unlike postcards of any other publisher. The numbering of the cards was quite complex, especially as it was consecutive only in certain ranges at one time. Although the firm did some black-and-white printing in their London offices, the majority of colour work was contracted for in Germany.

Tuck ran very successful postcard competitions through the early 1900s with prizes offered for the largest collection of Tuck cards sent through the post. In the first competition, the first prize of £1000 was awarded to the collector of 20,364 cards, a massive total to amass over the 18-month duration of the competition. Events such as these along with sales impetus in the firm helped foster the postcard boom during the 1900s. It also changed the focus to the "collectors of Tuck postcards" rather than the artists whose work was depicted.

In 1903, the firm moved into the five-storeyed "Raphael House" to house all the departments of their art business. On 29 December 1940, however, in one of the worst air raids of the Second World War, Raphael House was bombed. Several original artworks and records were destroyed. Fortunately, millions of cards had left the building over the previous years and their distribution throughout the "wide wide world" has kept them preserved with the collectors.

Raphael Tuck's grandson, Desmond Tuck, the last member of the Tuck family to have any connection with the firm, retired in 1959. The firm was taken over in 1962 by Purnell & Sons Ltd. In 1972, The Fine Art Developments Ltd., Europe's largest greetings card manufacturers and distributors purchased the company. The company became the British Printing & Communications Corporation in

1982, and Maxwell Communications Corporation in 1987, which was originally located only at a short distance from where the first shop of Raphael Tuck once stood. Maxwell Corporation was disestablished in 1991 with its properties sold to various media companies.

Del Tufo & Co., Madras (1890–1910s)
Publisher

Del Tufo & Co. was one of the early publishers of undivided-back picture postcards of Seringapatam, Madras, and other sights in the Madras Presidency, such as Madurai and Mahabalipuram.

Ravi Varma Fine Art Lithographic Press (Est. 1894)
Printer

The renowned artist Raja Ravi Varma (1848–1906) was born in Kilimanoor in the erstwhile princely state of Travancore. In the 1860s, the young Ravi Varma moved to the court of Maharaja Ayilyam Thirunal at Travancore, where he had the opportunity to observe and train under European and Indian court painters, using both oils and watercolours. He studied albums of European paintings, including Edward Moor's *Hindu Pantheon* published in 1810.

These early influences had a deep impact on the artist's style — he aesthetically blended the newest European art techniques of the time with Indian sensibilities, becoming well known throughout the country for his poetic representation of women and his dramatic visualisation of the Hindu epics and mythology, creating the first realist images of the gods that are being replicated till date. In the 1870s, early on in his journey as an artist, Ravi Varma exhibited his works at Madras, Vienna, London and Chicago, winning numerous medals for his work. Later in 1904, Lord Curzon awarded him with the Kaiser-i-Hind medal.

In 1888, the acclaimed artist was invited to meet the Gaekwad of Baroda while he was vacationing in Ooty and was commissioned by him to make fifteen large oil paintings depicting scenes from the Ramayana and Mahabharata for the Durbar Hall at his newly built Laxmi Vilas Palace. Ravi Varma completed these paintings by 1890. The artworks were first exhibited in Trivandrum, followed by Bombay and Baroda, for viewing by members of the public before being installed at the Durbar Hall of the palace.

The same year, for the first time, mass produced images of this "Baroda series" appeared in the form of photographic prints that were purchased extensively by people all over the country. After Raja Ravi Varma's death in 1906, these photographic images were put together in 1911 by S.N. Joshi in the booklet "Half Tone Reprints of the Renowned Pictures of the late Raja Ravi Varma", published by the Chitrashala Steam Press, Poona.

In the late 19th century, Calcutta, Bombay and Poona were the main centres of printed image production in India. On the advice of T. Madhava Rao, the former Dewan of Travancore and later Baroda, Ravi Varma founded his lithographic press in Girgaum, Bombay, in 1894 in partnership with a local entrepreneur named Govardhandas Khataumakhanji and with the assistance of German technicians. Bombay was strategically chosen as a location to facilitate ease of importing machinery from Germany and distributing the prints. Soon enough the printing press set new standards in the size, print quality and tactility of the images. In that era of increased nationalist sentiment, Ravi Varma's "Calendar Art" or popular mass-produced chromolithographs helped increase the involvement of common people with fine art across the country. It helped forge a national identity, and they were inspired by this unified visual culture in depicting Hindu mythology. Many a times, the figures in his prints were appropriated at a personal and domestic level by "dressing them up" with brocade cloth and the application of sequins and glitter. Simultaneously, he found patronage from European clients, who admired his mastery over Western portraiture technicalities.

In 1901, Ravi Varma sold his stake in the press and the copyright of 89 paintings to Fritz Schleicher, the German technician who was working with him. Ravi Varma detached himself entirely from functioning of the press by 1903. Thereafter the press moved out of Bombay to Malavali near Lonavala, a town on the Bombay to Poona railway line. The press continued to issue prints by other artists such as V.M. Dhurandhar, M.A. Joshi and Naoroji, all with Ravi Varma's signature. Unfortunately, the press burnt down in a fire accident later.

Weltreise Verlag Compagnie Comet (Fr. Th & Co.), Dresden
Publisher

Founded by Peter May Verlag, the firm published distinctive "Souvenir of East Indies" postcards and also larger colour offset litho prints in the 20 x 28 inch size. Their postcards comprise some of the earliest postcards of India, depicting Indian street scenes, historic sights, native people and their rituals.

H.W. West, Coonoor
Publisher

Published numerous postcards of the Nilgiri Railways and Coonoor.

Wiele & Klein, Madras (1882–1960s)
Commercial Photographer

This highly acclaimed studio was established in Madras by the German photographers E.F.H. Wiele and Theodore Klein. For a few years, they operated a second Branch in Ootacamund.

Wiele & Klein photographed several significant events, including the Coronation of King Edward VII and his wife Queen Alexandra. Over 200 lithographed photographs taken at the coronation and a set of picture postcards, all duly marked, were put together in a large, luxurious album titled *The Coronation Durbar Delhi 1903*. The studio also photographed the weddings in the Wadiyar family of Mysore. Around 1904, Wiele & Klein produced nearly 500 picture postcards using their own photographs. The albumen paper used by the studio was completely replaced by glossy silver gelatine paper. Most of Wiele & Klein's postcards were printed in Saxony. The firm allowed publishers in Bombay and Calcutta to use their photographs for picture postcards for a high fee.

Their postcards captured the prominent attractions of Madras and other sights in the presidency—landscapes, temples, rural views and the people.

Wiele & Klein was also known for their Cabinet Cards issued "By Appointment to His Excellency, The Governor of Madras." They also produced a set of stereographs, which were coined "Veritagrammes" and compiled in a set called the "Indian Series".

Wiele & Klein received numerous awards between 1890–1893. This photographic studio also finds mention in the 1914 edition of *Baedeker's Indien*. The photographer Fred Bremner also mentioned the German photographers in his memoir *My Forty Years in India*.

With Wiele establishing his own studio in Bangalore in 1908, the firm became Klein and Peyerl in 1926.

Many of their prints are now part of the photo archives of the Vintage Vignettes collection in Madras and the Volkerkunde Museum (Ethnology Museum) of Heidelberg.

Ad. Wiesenfeld, Hamburg
Publisher

Several undivided-back postcards of Indian cities, including Bombay, Calcutta and Agra, were published by this German publisher in and around the year 1900.

C.A Wiles, Brighton (1920s)
Photographer

A photographer from Brighton, C.A. Wiles captured events such as the unveiling of the Indian Memorial Gateway by the Maharaja of Patiala in Punjab, and the "Unveiling of the Chattri" on the Downs Patcham by the Prince of Wales in 1921.

Wochenpost

Wochenpost or *The Weekly Post* was a popular illustrated magazine from Austria. They also published picture postcards using exotic images from round the world.

W.R.B & Co., Vienna
Publisher

W.R.B & Co. published a variety of fine art, topographical and ethnographical picture postcards during the 1910s–1920s. They also published postcards of the artworks of the famous Austrian landscape painter Ludwig Hans Fischer. All their postcards were numbered.

BIBLIOGRAPHY

Allen, Charles. *Raj: A Scrapbook of British India: 1877–1947*. New Delhi: Indian Book Company, 1977.

Babb, Lawrence A., and Susan S. Wadley, eds., *Media and the Transformation of Religion in South Asia*. Philadelphia: University of Pennsylvania Press, 1995.

Bartholomew, J.G. *Constable's Hand Atlas of India*. London: Archibald Constable & Company, 1893.

[Bengal–Nagpur Railway]. *Travel in India or City, Shrine, and Sea Beach: Antiquities, Health and Places of Interest on the Bengal–Nagpur Railway*. Bombay: The Times Press, 1916.

Berger, John. *Ways of Seeing*. London: Penguin Books, 2008.

Betts, Vanessa and Victoria McCulloch. *Delhi & Northwest India*. Bath: Footprint Travel Guides, 2014.

Bourne, Samuel. *Photographic Journeys in the Himalayas, 1863–1866*. Compiled and edited by Hugh Rayner. Bath: Pagoda Tree Press, 2009.

Byatt, Anthony. *Picture Postcards and Their Publishers: An Illustrated Account Identifying Britain's Major Postcard Publishers, 1894–1939, and the Great Variety of Cards They Issued*. Malvern, Worcestershire: Golden Age Postcard Books, 1978.

Caine, W.S. *Picturesque India*. London: George Routledge & Sons Limited, 1891.

Charney, Michael W. *A History of Modern Burma*. Cambridge: Cambridge University Press, 2009.

Dadha, M. Maher. *Views of India: Connoisseurs Compendium, Art of the British Raj*. Bangalore: Dukan, 2000.

Davis, Bonnie. *Postcards of Old Siam*. Singapore: Marshall Cavendish, 2012.

Desmond, Ray. *Victorian India in Focus*: *A Selection of Early Photographs from the Collection in the India Office Library and Records*. London: Her Majesty's Stationary Office, 1982.

Falconer, John. *India: Pioneering Photographers, 1850-1900*. London: The British Library Publishing Division, 2001.

Filip, Vladimir. *Brno: Old Postcards*. Brno, Czech Republic: Josef Filip Publishing House, 2007.

Gaenszle, Martin and Jörg Gengnagel, eds. *Visualising Space in Banaras: Images, Maps and the Practice of Representation*. Wiesbaden: Harrassowitz Publishing House, 2006.

Gandhi, Mahatma. *Mahatma Gandhi & the Railways*, Compiled and edited by Y.P. Anand. Ahmedabad: Navajivan Trust, 2011.

Gilpin, William. *Three Essays: On Picturesque Beauty, On Picturesque Travel and on Sketching Landscape: To Which is Added a Poem, on Landscape Painting*. London: R. Blamire, 1792.

Godrej, Pheroza, and Pauline Rohatgi. *Scenic Splendours: India Through The Printed Image*. London: The British Library, Arnold Publishers, 1989.

Gutman, Judith Mara. *Through Indian Eyes: 19th and Early 20th Century Photography from India*. New York: Oxford University Press, 1982.

Haks, Leo and Steven Wachlin. *Indonesia: 500 Early Postcards*. Singapore: Editions Didier Millet, 2004.

'Hijrat Movement (1920)'*, historypak.com,* March 13, 2014, http://historypak.com/hijrat-movement-1920

Jhingan, Madhukar. *Postcard Catalogue: India and Indian States 1879–1979*. New Delhi: We Philatelists, 1979.

Kaufmann, Walter. *Life at the Limits*. New York: Reader's Digest Press, 1978.

Kaufmann, Walter. *Time is an Artist*. New York: Reader's Digest Press, 1978.

Khan, K.D.L. 'Much More Than a Bookstore.' *The Tribune,* Spectrum, October 23, 2005. http://

www.tribuneindia.com/2005/20051023/spectrum/main2.htm

Klich, Lynda and Benjamin Weiss. *The Postcard Age*: *Selections from the Leonard A. Lauder Collection*. London: Thames & Hudson, 2012.

Kollin, Ferenc. *Greetings from Old Budapest*. Translated by Ildiko Hann. Budapest: Corvina, 1988.

Landwehr, Gabrielle. 'The German Photographers of Madras.' *Madras Musings* 18, no. 14 (November 1–15, 2008), http://madrasmusings.com/Vol%2018%20No%2014/the_german_ photographers_of_madras.html

Mathur, Saloni. *India by Design: Colonial History and Cultural Display*. New Delhi: Orient Blackswan Private Limited, 2011.

McLeod Frances. 'Dr Montague's Siblings Elizabeth and Julian Rust.' *genealogy.com*, February 4, 2017, http://genforum.genealogy.com/rust/messages/1025.html

Miedema, Virgil and Stephanie Miedema. *Mussoorie and Landour: Footprints of the Past*. New Delhi: Rupa, 2014.

Montague, Joel G. *Picture Postcards of Cambodia: 1900–1950*. Bangkok: White Lotus, 2010.

Mundy, Godfrey Charles. *Pen and Pencil Sketches: Being the Journal of a Tour in India*, Volume 1 and 2. London: John Murray, 1832.

Murray, John. *A Handbook for Travellers in India, Burma & Ceylon*, 7th edition. London: John Murray, 1909.

Murray, John. *A Handbook for Travellers in India, Burma & Ceylon,* 18th edition. Edited by Arthur C. Lothian. London: John Murray, 1959.

Muthiah, S. 'Printers' Ink on Mount Road.' *The Hindu,* Metro Plus, August 13, 2003, Chennai edition, http://www.thehindu.com/thehindu/mp/2003/08/13/stories/2003081300140300.htm

Orian, Edmund, ed. *Prague in Picture Postcards of the Period 1886–1930*. Prague: Belle Epoque, 1998.

Osborne, Charles. *The Opera House Album: A Collection of Turn of the Century Postcards*. London: Robson Books, 1979.

Panter-Downes, Mollie. *Ooty Preserved: A Victorian Hill Station in India*. London: Century Publishing, 1967.

Parthasarathy, Shruti. 'Romancing the Camera.' *The Hindu,* Sunday Magazine, November 7, 2004, http://www.thehindu.com/thehindu/mag/2004/11/07/stories/2004110700520500.htm

Pinney, Christopher. *Camera Indica: The Social Life of Indian Photographs.* London: Reaktion Books, 1997.

Pinney, Christopher. '*Photos of the Gods': The Printed Image and Political Struggle in India.* London: Reaktion Books, 2004.

Pinney, Christopher. *The Coming of Photography in India.* London: The British Library, 2008.

Rao, M.A. *Indian Railways.* (India – The Land and People Series). New Delhi: National Book Trust, 1975.

Raza, Rosemary. *Representing Sindh: Images of the British Encounter.* Mumbai: Marg Publications, 2014.

Reshii, Marryam H. 'Views from Kashmir.' *Business Standard*, June 3, 2006, http://www.business-standard.com/article/beyond-business/views-from-kashmir-106060301006_1.html

Rohatgi, Pauline and Pheroza Godrej, eds. *India: A Pageant of Prints.* Mumbai: Marg Publications, 1989.

Rohatgi, Pauline and Pheroza Godrej, eds. *Under the Indian Sun: British Landscape Artists.* Mumbai: Marg Publications, 1995.

Satow, Michael, and Ray Desmond. *Railways of the Raj.* London: Scolar Press, 1982.

Schivelbusch, Wolfgang. *The Railway Journey: The Industrialization of Time and Space in the 19th Century.* Oakland: University of California Press, 1987.

Sharma, Neena. 'Doon Through the Lens.' *The Tribune*, Dehradun Plus, August 19, 2009, http://www.tribuneindia.com/2009/20090819/dplus.htm

Singh, Saint Nihal. *India Beckons.* Bombay: Publicity Department, Great Indian Peninsula Railway, c. 1930s.

Singh, Saint Nihal. *The Road to India's Past.* Bombay: Publicity Department, Great Indian Peninsula Railway, c. 1930s.

Soofi, Mayank Austen. 'Mahatta & Co: The Original Photoshop.' *Livemint*, June 20, 2015, https://www.livemint.com/Leisure/15o0JIEzCeihkxX5mlVBXN/Mahatta--Co-The-original-photoshop.html

Srikumar, S. *Kolar Gold Fields: Unfolding the Untold.* Gurgaon: Partridge Publishing, 2014.

Sriram, V. 'A Home to Literature.' *The Hindu,* Metro Plus, January 16, 2015, http://www.thehindu.com/features/metroplus/hidden-histories-a-home-to-literature/article6793737.ece

Staff, Frank. *The Picture Postcard and its Origins.* New York: Frederick A. Praeger Publishers, 1967.

The Earl Mountbatten of Burma. Introduction to *The Last Empire: Photography in British India, 1855-1911* by Clark Worswick and Ainslie Embree. New Delhi: Timeless Books, 1976.

[The Hindu]. 'When the Postman Knocked...' *The Hindu,* Metro Plus, May 20, 2013, http://www.thehindu.com/todays-paper/tp-features/tp-metroplus/when-the-postman-knocked/article4731513.ece

The Times, India Number, London, February 18, 1930.

The Times, India Number, London, March 23, 1937.

The Times, Weekly Edition, London, Thursday, June 29, 1933.

The Travellers' Guide to South India. Trichinopoly: Chief Commercial Superintendent, South Indian Railway, c. 1940.

[Thomas Cook & Son]. *India, Burma and Ceylon: Information for Travellers and Residents.* London: Thomas Cook & Son, 1923.

Urwick, W. *India Illustrated: With Pen and Pencil.* New York: Hurst & Company, 1891

White, Bridget. *Kolar Gold Fields – Down Memory Lane: Paeans to Lost Glory!* Bloomington: Author House, 2010.

Yule, Henry and A. C. Burnell. *Hobson-Jobson*: *A Glossary of Colloquial Anglo-Indian Words and Phrases, and of Kindred Terms, Etymological, Historical, Geographical and Discursive.* Edited by William Crooke. London: John Murray, 1903.

INDEX